# MAKING AND TAKING
# CAREER CHANGES

## BRITISH COAL ENTERPRISE LTD

BCE was formed at the end of 1984 to create new job opportunities in coal mining areas. So successful has it been that unemployment has for some time been falling faster in the coalfields than elsewhere – despite the challenge posed by 120,000 colliery job losses in five years. This success has been noticed by many other companies, who have employed BCE to act on their behalf through Job Shops, Self-Marketing Workshops and other means in order to lessen the personal difficulties caused by redundancy. As a result, BCE is now Britain's largest outplacement company, and its knowledge of the techniques needed in building a new career is second to none. This book provides much of that knowledge in a most readable form.

# JOHN LYNCH
# MAKING AND TAKING
# CAREER CHANGES

## A BRITISH COAL ENTERPRISE HANDBOOK

**British COAL enterprise**

**PANDON PRESS**

Copyright © British Coal Enterprise 1990, 1991.

ISBN: 1 85557 003 3

First published 1991 by
British Coal Enterprise Limited,
Edwinstowe House,
Edwinstowe,
Mansfield,
Nottinghamshire NG21 9PR,
*in association with*
Pandon Press Limited,
P.O. Box 1SN,
Newcastle upon Tyne NE99 1SN

*Making and Taking Career Changes* is a revised
edition of the *Career Development Handbook*
published by British Coal Enterprise in 1990.

Designed & produced by Pandon Press Limited, Newcastle upon Tyne.

Printed in Great Britain by
Billing & Sons Limited, Worcester.

# CONTENTS

INTRODUCTION: *Why are you reading this?*
7    Reasons for change

CHAPTER 1: *The redundant executive – how does it feel?*
8    Psychological impact of redundancy
9    You have to do it yourself
9    The job-seeker as salesperson
10   Time is not on your side

CHAPTER 2: *The job-hunter – a question of attitude*
11   People do not buy on rational grounds
12   Positive Mental Attitude
12   Keeping the tools of your trade in order

CHAPTER 3: *Same again?*
14   Life is not a dress rehearsal
14   Reasons for change
15   Stages in life
16   The satisfactions you get from work
17   Change to what?
18   Self-employment
20   Voluntary work
21   Intensive pursuit of a hobby, paid or otherwise
21   Further education

CHAPTER 4: *Who are you?*
22   Self-analysis
25   Psychometric tests

CHAPTER 5: *How am I placed?*
31   Personal financial analysis
35   Cash flow forecast
36   Balance sheet

CHAPTER 6: *Finding a job*
38    The sources of jobs
38    Networking
39    Press advertisements
46    Speculative approach by the candidate
51    Headhunters and recruitment consultants

CHAPTER 7: *CVs – How to tell your life story*
55    CVs are not about responsibilities and lists of jobs
55    CV form and content
57    Features, not benefits
58    Alternative CV models
60    "Housekeeping" details
62    Writing your history
63    Other approaches
66    Good English
71    CVs – summary

CHAPTER 8: *Going for it – How to excel in interviews*
72    Job interviews are selling interviews
72    Research
74    Conducting the interview
77    Common lines of questioning
81    Your own questions
82    Asking for the job
83    Interview Technique – Summary

CHAPTER 9: *Working for yourself*
84    Overtrading
96    Business Plan Questionnaire

CHAPTER 10: *Management Buyouts and Buyins*
98    Management buyouts and buyins

CHAPTER 11: *Voluntary work*
103    The range of possibilities

CHAPTER 12: *Further Education*
105    Further education

107    APPENDIX ONE: *Sources of funds for business*
115    APPENDIX TWO: *Useful addresses*
119    INDEX

# INTRODUCTION

## *Why are you reading this?*

This is a career development book with a difference. It is designed for men and women of executive status who are looking for a new way to live their lives.

Now, there are several reasons why you may be contemplating this change and several things you may be thinking of changing to. You may, for example, be redundant; you may be working but bored with your job; or you may feel that you have potential for a fuller, more satisfying life that is not going to be realised as long as you stay where you are. You may wish to find a new job in the line in which you are trained and experienced; you may want to take on something entirely new to you; you may have an interest or hobby that you now wish to pursue on a full-time basis; you may want to go into business for yourself.

There are other possibilities. Whatever your own case may be, we shall try to deal with it in this book. Thus, Chapter 1 is called *The redundant executive. How does it feel?*, and deals with the psychological position of the redundant executive. Chapter 2 is addressed to the person who wishes to feel more fulfilled. Other chapters tell you how to put your chosen course into action.

It will be clear, then, that not all of the book can possibly be relevant to you. Select those parts that *are* relevant. Whatever it is that motivates you, and whatever you want to do, we believe that you will find the advice you need within these pages.

Life should not be boring. It should not be a treadmill. It should be a source of joy, and satisfaction, and pride. We hope that we can help you find these benefits in your own life.

One more thing. I am well aware that words can influence the way we think about things and that language is inherently sexist. I have tried to avoid sexist writing in this book; where I have failed, please forgive me. If I have inadvertently used words like 'man' and 'he', please read 'person' or 's/he'.

Good luck!

# CHAPTER 1

## *The redundant executive. How does it feel?*

In one of Tom Sharpe's comic novels, a woman whose child has been abducted is approached by the press. How, a typically insensitive reporter wants to know, does it feel to be in this position? The mother attacks the journalist with her handbag and with her feet, leaving him a bruised and sorry mess on the floor.

'It feels,' she tells him, 'like that'.

And so does losing one's job feel like that. We may not have been surprised when the axe fell; we may be pleased with the financial arrangements; we may even have been unhappy with the company and already looking for a move. Nevertheless, redundancy is rejection; it is experienced as rejection and it can never be felt as anything but rejection. And rejection, cutting as it does at our sense of self-worth, is not a nice experience.

We have talked to a lot of redundant executives; and because people vary in temperament, in training and in background, the views we heard differed. Two things, though, came up again and again.

The first was that redundancy is like bereavement; like the loss of a close family member. The second related to the value that our society places on work. To lose one's job, we were told, was to lose one's self-respect. Redundant executives felt ashamed.

If you are to survive redundancy properly, there are two things that you must do. You must rise above it – but you must first experience it without evasion; you must mourn what is lost, just as you would mourn the bereavement to which redundancy is so often likened. In the specific case of rejection-as-redundancy, you must mourn the job that is gone.

What non-British twaddle, we hear you say, and it is certainly true that mourning is not something the British do well. This is true of British men in particular, and as men still make up the huge majority of executives, we believe that most are going to need this advice.

You are not going to be ready to move on in a healthy state of mind until you have:

Grieved for the job you have lost; the job itself, the status it carried, the relationships it offered; *and*

Allowed your natural anger at being rejected to come to the surface and to take its course.

We are thinking here, of course, of forms of expression that fall short of taking a gun to the person who fired you; or of the kinds of harassment that can damage your opportunities of finding other work.

So it is all right to be angry; it is all right to feel resentment; it is all right to believe that you have been harshly treated. Most of all, it is all right to cry. In the words of an American song of the sixties, crying lets the sad out of you. The British taboo on men crying has meant that British men are unable to deal with anguish in a healthy way.

Psychologists recognise five stages in the mourning process:

- Denial (I don't believe that this is happening to me);
- Bargaining (If I do *x*, you won't have to fire me/she won't have left me/he won't really be dead);
- Anger;
- Depression;
- Acceptance.

These stages may overlap, and they will vary in length for different people, but you have not mourned properly until you have experienced and lived through each one of them. There are no short cuts.

When the mourning is properly over, you will be in much better mental health, and much more able to go about finding and starting a new job, in a sane and productive way. And this is where the 'rising above' comes in.

You are out of work. You have been rejected. You are not the first. You have talent, you have skills, because if you did not have these things, you would not have reached the position you occupied in the first place. Perhaps you find yourself doubting your talent and your skills – if so, you probably have not mourned properly – but you do have them. What you have to do now is what countless people have had to do before you. You have to find a new job.

This book aims to help you, and that word *help* is very important. You have to do the job *yourself*. We can help you look inside yourself and identify, in order to overcome, the feelings of rejection. We can show you how to analyse your strengths and weaknesses; how to decide what you want to do next; how to look for openings in that sphere; how to prepare for the selection process and how to conduct yourself during it; but we cannot find a job for you, or land it for you. And neither can anyone else. *You have to do it yourself.*

A small number of you – let us say, ten per cent – are salespeople. You are the lucky ones. Not because sales jobs are easier than others to find –

at the level at which you are looking, they are not – but because you have developed a number of the skills and attitudes that redundant executives need. The others are going to have to acquire some of them.

Salespeople are used to rejection. The best salesperson in the world hears 'no' more often than 'yes'. They therefore find the emotional pain of redundancy that much easier to take – not easy, but less difficult.

Salespeople are used to selling things, and that is what every redundant executive reading this is now going to have to do – and the product you are selling is nothing less than yourselves.

So, a lot of this book is going to be about applying marketing and selling techniques to a unique product – yourself.

Before we move on to Chapter 2, a word about time. It is not on your side. The first edition (1990) of this book quoted a recent American study which suggested that finding a new job took one month for every £7,000 of salary required. That was only a year ago, but things are getting tougher. British research says that it may now (mid-1991) take a year or more for the £50,000 p.a. job-seeker to be settled.

We asked you earlier how it felt. Well, it is probably going to feel worse. Competition for new jobs is fierce, and you are likely to experience many moments of depression before you land one. You will be tempted to despair. Don't. If – and we are going to help – you form a clear view at the outset of what your capabilities are and what your potential is, and if you then set to work marketing yourself as we will show you, then *you will find another job*. It may take time, but it *will happen*.

# CHAPTER 2

# *The job-hunter – a question of attitude*

People do not buy on rational grounds. Salespeople take *this* order because they took the last one. Unsuccessful salespeople rapidly begin to project the idea, 'I'm not going to win this', so that, even if they have the right product, the prospect thinks, 'S/he must know more than I do – I'd better not buy from her/him'. By contrast, salespeople who really do expect to get the order convey that expectation, if subliminally, and with it the idea that theirs is the right product for the job.

Of course, there may be other salespeople showing equal confidence, and so the person who does expect to win may still not do so; but if this order does not come in, another will.

What has this to do with you, the redundant person? This: that you are, for now, a salesperson; that the product you are offering is yourself; and that you must therefore cultivate an air of confidence in your rightness for whatever job you are going after, and of certainty that it will be offered to you. It is, as the chapter heading says, a question of attitude.

Now, that confident attitude will sometimes be difficult to sustain. You are marketing yourself in a harshly competitive world; a world where, as things stand at present, the buyer holds most of the cards. Your spirits will rise when your contacts promise help, only to be dashed when the promise comes to nothing. Recruitment consultants will dangle jobs in front of you, jobs that you know you are perfectly qualified for, and after a few days or several weeks you will learn that the consultant's brief has changed, that a more suitable applicant has come forward, or that the consultant had not been retained to fill that post in the first place. An offer will be promised to you, only for a headcount freeze to be imposed before it can be issued. You will go for interviews at which you never get going, never show yourself in the most favourable light, because you relate poorly to the interviewer, or because you cannot understand her or his line of questioning, or the way in which it is delivered.

And still, you have to maintain your confidence. How on earth are you to do it?

Well, how do salespeople do it – these people who hear 'no' more often than 'yes'? They live in a world of constant rejection. Prospects refuse to see them. People who want what they have to offer cannot get budget approval. Entrenched competitors beat them on price, on function, on delivery. Demonstration units fail to turn up, or to work when they do get there. Orders that were promised, all but in the bag, fail at the last minute to materialise. And still they get up every morning, pick up their bags and drive off to do battle again – and to face more rejection.

How do they do it, these paragons? They have three main methods.

First, they cultivate something they call PMA – Positive Mental Attitude. You will meet few salespeople who cannot tell you what PMA is. This is, of course, a circular argument: salespeople avoid being negative by being positive; they do it by doing it. Nevertheless, PMA is as real as NMA – Negative Mental Attitude – and a good deal less common among people who have been out of work for a while. You are going to have an attitude – your mind is not going to be empty – and you can choose whether it is positive or negative. Oh yes, you can. Many people challenge this; but if you want to, you can put the defeats, the disappointments, the poor interviews behind you as soon as you recognise them for what they are. You can choose to tell yourself: I made a mistake, and I have learned from it. I will not make the same mistake again.

Tell yourself also: I have talent. I am able. I succeeded before because I deserved to succeed, and I shall succeed again. There is a job for me, and it *is* the right job, and I *will* get it. It may take some time, but I *will* get it.

The second thing salespeople do is to keep the tools of their trade in order. They practise interviewing technique. They research the companies they intend to call on. They look for more companies to call on. They always arrive early, and they are always well and appropriately dressed. We will spend quite a lot of time on this course teaching you how to do these things as well as the salesperson does.

And the third thing salespeople do is this: they get by with a little help from their friends. Selling is a lonely game. So is looking for work. Again and again, salespeople's colleagues pick them up when they are down, remind them of their abilities and successes, and send them out again looking for more. You, the redundant executive, need the same sort of support.

This is why Job Clubs have become so popular – not because misery loves company; and not, or at least, not only, because Benefit entitlements may be tied to attendance; but because redundancy is lonely, and other people help to make it less so.

Do not allow your shame at being unemployed to drive you away from those who are still at work. Ideally, recognise that there is no shame attached to being unemployed in the nineteen nineties; but, if you cannot do that, overcome it to the point of not cutting yourself off. You need friendship; you need help; you need contact with those who are still in work. You need, above all, to maintain faith in your value as a human being.

In Chapter 3, we are going to talk about the world you have entered and about the position you want to take up in it. You may decide on more of the same – employment with a new company in the same kind of job that you were doing previously. You may decide that it is time for a complete change. Whatever choice you make, remember that statistics are encouraging – in the long run. The great majority of those who become redundant find work again. And so will you. If you follow the advice in this book.

It is all a question of attitude.

## CHAPTER 3

# *Same again?*

There is a well-known joke about opportunities and problems. Is the joke close to life? You are redundant. Life, it seems, has played you a nasty trick; but has it, in fact, offered you a disguised opportunity? Is this the time to stop living your life the way you have been living it, and find a life-style you like better?

Life is, after all, not a dress rehearsal. We have only one; and, as Larkin reminded us, whether or not we use it, it goes.

Many people do want to change the way they live; but because people vary, the reasons vary. Yours may be:

- To make money.
- To overcome boredom.
- To obtain a greater sense of self-worth.
- To fulfil a long-cherished dream.
- An external impetus, such as redundancy or early retirement.

or it may be something entirely different. Perhaps you would have come to the decision to change anyway. Now that you are redundant, or looking for new openings for some other reason, the message must be to turn this outside force into an advantage. An optimist has been described as someone who sees a glass half full, while a pessimist sees it half empty. When a change is forced upon him, the optimist will seek to benefit from it. Is this you?

## Reasons for change

There are, in fact, good reasons why the idea of change is more often thought of today than by earlier generations. We are different from our parents. The executive, redundant or otherwise, to whom this book is addressed may be middle-aged; or may not yet have reached that point. Middle-aged people today are from the first generation to enjoy free secondary education. They have developed personal resources denied to their forebears: they have enjoyed travel, cultural and leisure activities that have expanded their ability to seize opportunities; they have often accumulated a net worth that, though modest by some standards, would have been unimaginable to their parents. They are better informed about the world through television, radio and newspapers as well as through travel. Those who are younger find it even more difficult to understand the limits that there were on life only forty years ago.

Some constraints remain. Most people still marry, or enter settled relationships. Most people still have children. More people divorce than used to. People still live in houses or flats, which they still furnish. There is, therefore, a period during which a steady cashflow must be generated, and for most people a steady cashflow means a steady job.

However, it is clear that life can be divided into a number of stages. For a given individual, these stages and the priorities they bring with them might look like this:

| AGE | STATE | PRIORITY |
| --- | --- | --- |
| Late teens/early 20s | Generally single | Leisure & self-enjoyment |
| Late 20s/late 30s | Newly married with children | Provision for family |
| Late 30s/late 40s | Children growing up; financially stable. | Scope to fulfil one's needs if that is |
| Late 40s onwards | | what one wants |

So where, in this model, are you? Are you ready to accept your present position as a turning point – a springboard to help you move into a rewarding, satisfying later life? Because career decisions taken years ago *can* be changed. If you want to, or feel the need to. New opportunities *can* be seized. Self-realisation – the fulfilment of *all* your potential – *can* be achieved. Is this the time?

If you *do* want to develop a strategy for a new life, take your time. Most people – through no fault of their own – drifted into what they are doing now. If the time for change is here, let us plan it better. Life is to be enjoyed.

There is increasing recognition that the employer does have a moral responsibility to help soften the jolt of redundancy. You may be reading this as part of an outplacement course arranged by your employers for that very reason. Nevertheless, the first responsibility for making the most of one's own life belongs with the individual. If at the end of her or his life a person feels that s/he has not achieved what she or he might have done, it will bring precious little satisfaction to blame others while knowing that s/he could have done better – and did not.

So you must look closely at what is going on in your mind, and decide whether you feel an impetus towards change. While you are thinking about that, look also at the satisfactions your work has given you. You will still need most of them. They are likely to have included:

- Money;
- Self-esteem;
- Peer group respect;
- A sense of belonging;
- Friends; *and*
- Conversation.

**Money** speaks for itself; the others possibly less so. Let us look at them in more detail. (A lot of what I am going to say may seem simple, and you may feel that it is written below your level. Please, read it anyway. One of the things we are trying to do is to help you come to terms with your situation; and stating the obvious may help get things into the open – and help you start that grieving process).

**Self-esteem.** It rarely occurs to us that our job gives us self-esteem; but the person out of work feels its loss. Our society is based on the concept of work, and we operate on the (perhaps unspoken) belief that what we do is more valuable than what we are. If we do nothing, we are worth nothing. This way of thinking may be wrong, but things that are wrong do not necessarily go away – and our research tells us that this loss of self-esteem hits many redundant executives hard.

**Peer group respect.** What makes being good at something really satisfying is the knowledge that *other people* know us to be good; and the most important other people in this context are the ones we work with.

**A sense of belonging.** Only true 'loners' do not need this, and there are very few of them. You may get it within your family, from clubs, or from your friends, but you are very likely also to get it at work.

**Friends.** You probably have many friends at work. They are work friends, and few of them are likely to stay close after you leave. Do you want to live without friends?

**Conversation.** We are social animals, and we need to talk to people. If you give up the conversation at your place of work, will you find a substitute?

Think about these qualities, and about which of them are most important to you, and take them into account when we start to deal with what you might want to change to. Your feelings will probably differ depending on whether or not you live alone; do you? What are the implications of that on your need to change what you are doing?

Do you want to move house? Perhaps you only live where you do because your present job demands it; perhaps you have always told yourself that, on the magic day when they handed you your gold watch and your first pension cheque, you would uproot yourself and set up home somewhere more attractive.

This can work, and it can also be a disaster. Moving on retirement to an isolated cottage in the Yorkshire Dales can leave you cut off from the satisfactions we outlined above, and the ensuing loneliness can take years off your life – or make it seem three times as long as it really is. Doing it in your twenties or thirties may be a wonderful thing to do, because you are likely to have children and children are the key to new friendships.

And moving in your middle years can also be tremendously rewarding. If you are going to be taking up a new way of life, and if you choose the right one for you, then you will make new friendships to replace those left behind.

Are you, in all this, considering your spouse's wishes? Does she or he really want to do what you want to do, or are you forcing it through? Does this reflect the way you have lived your lives in the past? Do you really think that that is a recipe for concord? Or even fair? Is one of you about to decide that the relationship is over? If so, have you thought through the financial impact (see Chapter 5)?

## Change to what?

If you know that you do not want, or cannot afford, to change the way you live, then you are no longer with us; you have moved on to the next section. Those who remain have thought about the reasons for change, and the need to make sure that they understood them. The next question is: what is it you want to change to?

You may already have some ideas about this. If so, look hard at them before committing yourself. This book is designed – or, at least, this part of it is – to help you realise your dreams; but some dreams are nightmares in disguise. Nothing now could possibly be more important than getting this decision right.

There are three questions we would like you to be thinking about as you read through the next few paragraphs. They are:

- What have you enjoyed about your life to date?
- What have you disliked?
- What emerged from the beginning of this chapter as your motivation for change?

Later on, we are going to spend some time developing an understanding of your strengths, your weaknesses, and how they affect what you can, and what you should not, do. For the moment, try a little lateral thinking. This is a technique that enables us to move from the obvious to the less obvious.

Here is an example.

A man with much experience in the sale of camping equipment was looking for ways to expand his interests. He asked himself the question: What business am I *really* in?; and found that his first answer – I am in the tent business – was inadequate. When he expanded that and said: I am in the business of providing opportunities for people to use their leisure time, a whole range of new opportunities suggested themselves.

That is lateral thinking.

So, when you go on to think about the skills that you have, try to think laterally in order to come up with alternative uses to which you can put them.

Now let us look at some of the choices available to you. What is the 'menu' from which you are going to be choosing? Chances are that, if you do want to change, it will be to something in one of the following categories:

- New, but different, employment;
- Self-employment (including consultancy or freelancing in your previous work);
- Voluntary work;
- Intensive pursuit of a hobby, paid or otherwise; *and/or*
- Further education.

**New employment.** Perhaps your choice is to continue in employment, but in a different field. You may make this choice because you need to continue to generate an income, or because you do not want to give up the satisfactions that work provides.

Are you already qualified for this new work? (See the relevant chapters to find out how to check what is required.) If you need training, we will also be telling you how to go about getting it.

Do you want to work full time? If not, how many hours each week would you like to work? Is this number likely to be acceptable to your potential employer?

There is an excellent book called *Second Chances for Adults,* which is probably available at your local reference library. Local Education Authorities have career services which provide a wide range of written information on what various jobs demand, and what they offer.

**Self-employment.** This is a dream for many people and, for most, a dream is what it should remain. Nothing requires more thought than the step into self-employment, because you are usually risking everything you have.

But self-employment may be the right thing for you. Many people have failed at it, but many have succeeded. If you can be one of the latter, it probably provides deeper and more varied satisfactions than anything else you can do outside the artistic sphere.

Getting to know your strengths and weaknesses is especially important if you are contemplating being your own boss, because you simply must have the qualities needed to succeed. What are these qualities? They are:

- Determination;
- Resilience;
- Resourcefulness;
- Self-sufficiency; *and*
- External support.

You will also need:

- Enough capital; *and*
- The right field to enter.

Let us look at these in turn.

**Determination.** You will be competing with established suppliers of whatever service or product you have decided to sell. Your competitors will not give ground lightly. Some customers will be unwilling to deal with a new, untested supplier; and some will want to take advantage of your newness, your desire to win business at any price, your ignorance of what margins are needed to enable you to survive. There are going to be many setbacks in the early days. Everyone has setbacks at work; but, in the last resort, these are the concern of the employer. Not in your case.

**Resilience.** When disappointments come, you have to accept them, pick yourself up and go after new sales. Further disappointments will come, and you will have to accept them, pick yourself up and go after new sales. And so on. And so on. This kind of resilience – the ability to keep taking setbacks, to keep picking yourself up – is not common. Are you sure you have it?

**Resourcefulness.** To run your own business, you will need to know or be able to find out many things. An awful lot of information and advice is available free, but you have to be the kind of person who can find out where to look.

**Enough capital.** We deal in Chapter 9 with the mechanics of making Business Plans and Cash Flow Forecasts. You will see that you are going to need sufficient capital to start up; to hold stocks, work in progress and finished goods; to wait for your customers to pay you; and to see you through whatever period of time it takes until the business is generating enough profit – in cash terms – to support you.

You will start out with a Business Plan, a Marketing Plan, a Cash Flow Forecast. As von Ludendorff said, 'No plan long survives contact with the enemy'. Your carefully laid plans will be blown off course, and when this happens you will have to change strategy on the run. Do you have what it takes to do this?

**Self-sufficiency.** As the previous paragraphs will have brought home, running your own business is your own responsibility. Successful entrepreneurs know how to harness the advice and assistance of others, but they also know where the buck stops, and they can handle it. Can you?

**External support.** Yes, you must be self-sufficient; but you must also be able to rely on the support of those around you – which means, essentially, your family.

A successful builder, who started with nothing and ended with a thriving business and quite rich, worked twelve hour days and seven-day weeks right through the early years. His wife raised their two children and looked after the house with no help from him. They both saw his success as their success, which is exactly what it was.

The Managing Director of what is now a large electronics company decided early in life that success in business was the greatest priority in his life. When his wife was unwilling to make the sacrifices described in the last paragraph, he divorced her. Some people are prepared to make that kind of sacrifice. Most are not. If you have the support of your partner – and if both of you have looked hard at what you plan to do, and what it will demand – the sacrifice is not required.

**The right field to enter.** You are going, with the help of this book, to get to know *you*; your strengths, your weaknesses, your special skills. This self-analysis, along with a little lateral thinking, will help you arrive at an idea of the sort of thing you can do.

It may be, though, that your plan to work for yourself is based around the fulfilment of a long cherished dream. Are you entirely sure that self-analysis carried out honestly does not show that you are, in fact, unsuited to that work?

For example, running a pub is one of Britain's commonest daydreams. Now, pubs continue in business, and the majority of them continue to make money, so the dream has clearly been translated into reality for many people – but many others have failed. If this is your dream, are you quite sure that you have the abilities which make running a pub both possible and satisfying – and are you sure that you lack the disabilities which rule it out?

**Voluntary work.** If you have no need to generate an income, but want to continue to experience the other satisfactions we listed in Chapter 2, then working for the good of others may be right for you. The Welfare State is not so all-encompassing that all of the needs of our society are or even can be met by full-time paid staff. There will always be a need for ordinary people to be involved.

Appendix 2 contains some addresses which will help you find the agency which needs precisely what you have to offer. One of the things that make this such a rich field for the experienced executive who seeks new opportunities is that the range of needs is enormous – all the way from people able and willing to engage in hard physical labour to those who can be trained to provide loving support to the bereaved. Examine your own talents in the light of this chapter, and decide what you could do.

**Intensive pursuit of a hobby, paid or otherwise**. You are financially secure enough not to need to work for money. Work has not been the only important thing in your life, and you have pursued a hobby at which you have become rather good. Now you want to stop working, and practise your hobby full-time.

This is one of the most rewarding things you can do, and if you really don't need an income from work, then the satisfactions that will come your way from pursuing your hobby are probably greater than those available anywhere else. Your hobby is what you love to do – if it were not, you would have stopped doing it. It must leave you more fulfilled than accountancy, or managing a factory. If you do have to make a financial sacrifice, you will probably feel that it is worth it.

Some questions, though. Will your partner and your family also feel that the sacrifice is justified? And, if the hobby keeps you at home, will they welcome you there? As a fixture, rather than an evening and weekend visitor? Are you sure?

**Further education**. There are still many executives who are not graduates. Perhaps your earlier life was devoted to qualifying in specialist disciplines which left no time for the other things you would like to know. Is it time to put that right? University is not only for the young; the number of mature students is growing. Nor need you feel restricted to the Open University – the particular pleasures that come from being part of a full-time, on-campus student body can still be enjoyed. Do not imagine that you will be the only mature student there – you won't.

The object of this chapter has been to get you thinking about whether you want to change the way you live, and why. It has, because it has had to, raised some questions; but only because we wanted you to be certain about your motivations for change. We do *not* want to urge change upon those who are happy as they are. We *do* want to suggest a springboard to help you move into a rewarding, satisfying later life.

This has been a diversion from the route of most approaches to redundancy, which assume that your only aim is to get back into full-time employment. We will now rejoin the others.

# CHAPTER 4

## *Who are you?*

If you are going to have to make decisions about what you want to do, you must understand yourself. Which means listing your strengths and weaknesses. In coming chapters, you are going to learn how to complete a cv, which is an account of your career to date – and that means listing what you have done so far. You are going to have to assess your financial position – and that means listing what you own, what you owe, and what income you are going to have.

The first such self-examination starts here.

It deals with who you are – what sort of person you are, and what sort of work you should be doing. When you have completed it, show it to people who know you – your spouse, friends you trust, a colleague or manager who has come to understand you well – and ask for their comments. You may be surprised. Few of us know ourselves as well as we may think we do; and the input of another person, received with understanding, can bring amazing insights into ourselves.

Let us be clear about what this exercise is not – it is not vocational guidance. By vocational guidance, I mean the sort of service that examines your career, your psychological makeup, your outside interests and your longstanding goals and desires, and then comes up with suggestions about the kind of work you may want to do.

There are agencies that practise vocational guidance, and some of them are very good. They work through psychometric tests, with discussion of the results, and through in-depth interviews. That should make it clear why we cannot offer vocational guidance in a book. It is a service that requires one-to-one counselling; and books don't talk.

You must therefore adopt a self-help approach. I take, as my starting-point, the conviction that the success of vocational guidance lies in its ability to bring out what the client already subconsciously knows.

The questionnaire you are about to complete deals with personal characteristics such as what gives – and what does not give – satisfaction; what provides – and what does not provide – motivation to work; what scares us and what we feel easy with. The answers to these questions can help us find out what way of life would suit the real us best.

This questionnaire is not a psychometric test. We will have more to say about psychometric tests when we deal with job search techniques, because headhunters and recruitment consultants use them extensively, and we will need to prepare you for them. They are designed to establish what kind of person you are, and the designers have perfected some remarkable techniques for achieving this aim. Tests measure a number of factors about you, and may show where you score on a continuum between two points. Thus, you may be rated for your position on the following lines:

Naive _____ Untrusting

Outgoing _____ Reserved

Self-confident _____ Lacking confidence

Team player_____ Loner

Leader _____ Follower

An insight into your psychological makeup organised in this way can be of enormous value in assessing the field in which you would be happiest – the field in which your natural characteristics would be most comfortably employed.

## The questionnaire

When you answer these questions, do so honestly. If you fool anyone, it can only be yourself. This is less easy than it sounds, for a number of reasons, one of which is that answering honestly involves thinking about the real you – not about the you that happens to be doing your present job.

For example, you may currently be employed in a job that requires you to deal with intricate detail, to co-operate with many colleagues, and to work in a large, open-plan office building. You may be very good at this work, enjoying the respect both of your peer group and of your superiors. And yet, you may know that your preferred work would involve consideration of the broad picture, with matters of detail delegated to others; you may be unhappy at having to relate to a workgroup of more than, say, four or five close colleagues; and you may long to be out on the road, visiting customers or suppliers, instead of spending your working day in an office.

These things do happen. In my own experience a good administrator became an even better salesman and rose to a Sales Director's position; a good salesman became an even better Personnel Manager; and a top flight secretary went into social work and blossomed.

Be aware, though, of the danger of wishful thinking. That administrator, good as he was, knew that he hated office work and that he needed the challenge of a sales territory, a less structured day, and targets to meet. The secretary had a deep need to help others in a positive way instead of ministering to the – as she saw it – less important requirements of middle managers, but it took psychometric tests and career counselling before she felt certain that she really did have the qualities needed for social work. The salesman had come to know himself and his talents in depth before deciding that the more academic, theoretical world of dealing with people as employees and colleagues rather than as prospects was for him.

So, you need to answer the questions on the basis of what you really know about yourself, and not on the basis of what you might wish you could do but probably cannot, or on the assumption that 'This is what I do now, and I do it well, so it must be what I do best'.

# WHO AM I?
## Self Analysis Questionnaire

*Note:* This is not a psychometric test, but an aid to self-analysis.

**What kind of work appeals most to you?** (*Tick all that apply*)
☐ Work that involves a great deal of detail
☐ Work that involves little detail
☐ Work that involves co-operation with others
☐ Work carried out mostly alone
☐ Work that carries pressing deadlines
☐ Work that can be completed in your own time

**What kind of work appeals least to you?** (*Tick all that apply*)
☐ Work that involves a great deal of detail
☐ Work that involves little detail
☐ Work that involves co-operation with others
☐ Work carried out mostly alone
☐ Work that carries pressing deadlines
☐ Work that can be completed in your own time

**What kind of work environment appeals most to you?**
(*Tick all that apply*)
☐ An open plan office
☐ Closed offices
☐ Work carried out at other firms' premises
☐ A constantly changing environment (e.g., 'on the road')
☐ Work at home
☐ A crowded, 'populated' environment
☐ A solitary, 'unpopulated' environment

**What kind of work environment appeals least to you?**
(*Tick all that apply*)
☐ An open plan office
☐ Closed offices
☐ Work carried out at other firms' premises
☐ A constantly changing environment (e.g., 'on the road')
☐ Work at home
☐ A crowded, 'populated' environment
☐ A solitary, 'unpopulated' environment

The following are benefits accruing from work. List them in their order of importance to you. Do not answer in relation to your present or last work, but to your ideal.

NOTE: *It is not necessary to assign a rating to every item on this list – just those that are important to you.*

☐ Money
☐ A structured day
☐ A structured environment
☐ Peer group respect
☐ Self-fulfilment
☐ Opportunity to be creative
☐ Companionship
☐ Friendship
☐ Conversation
☐ Opportunities for promotion
☐ Consciousness of bringing benefits to others
☐ Authority
☐ Self-respect

**What aspect of your present or last job has given you most pleasure?**

**What aspect of your present or last job has given you least pleasure?**

**What kind of worker would you most like to be?**

Why?

Have you a long-standing dream of the kind of work you would like to do?

What is it?

Why did you get into your present work?

Would you choose it again?

Why / Why not?

Now that you have answered the questions, we will not be attempting to tell you what your answers suggest would be the right job for you. This is, remember, a self-help exercise. You have established a number of things:

- Those aspects of work that attract you
- Those aspects of work that repel you
- The kind of environment you prefer to work in
- The kind of environment you prefer not to work in
- The benefits provided by work that are most important to you.

Look closely at the combination of factors you have isolated. You may spot some interesting connections.

Suppose, for example, that you said that *Work carried out mostly alone* is not attractive to you? Now take a look at the section in which you rated the benefits accruing from work in order of their importance to you. How did you score Peer Group Respect, Companionship, Friendship and Conversation? When we began carrying out these exercises, we were struck by the number of people who placed little value on these things, while not wanting to work alone.

There are two likely explanations. One is that some of those who answered in this way were not used to thinking of companionship, friendship and conversation as things they went to work for. It is quite likely, though, that they would miss them if they were taken away.

And the other possible explanation is that these people did not want to be alone – but that simply having others around was enough; they did not need (or even want) to talk much to them.

This simple example will show how you can draw conclusions from the answers you have produced.

Another thing you should be aware of is that your answers represent your feelings *at one moment in time*. People who administer psychometric tests know that one person's results can change dramatically over time. Changing jobs is a stressful time; doing it through redundancy is even more so. What you believe is most important may not, in fact, seem so next year.

Think of the factors emerging from your questionnaire as, together, making up a profile of the work that will give you most satisfaction. Now draw up your Profile on the form provided. Give this exercise plenty of time – not less, we would suggest, than one hour – and approach it *honestly*. Do not give in to the temptation merely to describe your present or last job as the ideal for you, or to assume that because you have always been an Accountant, an Accountant is what Providence meant you to be. Perhaps the fact that you have always been an Accountant and the fact that you are known to be irritable and unapproachable are not altogether unconnected?

# PERSONAL PROFILE

You have already completed a questionnaire that examined your strengths, weaknesses, likes and dislikes.

From this information, prepare a Personal Profile that lists the attributes your ideal job should have, and those it should definitely avoid.

**Describe the physical characteristics** (*indoors or out; closed/open plan; on others' premises; on the road, etc*) **that your ideal work would offer**

**Describe the physical characteristics that would not be present in your ideal work**

**Describe the satisfactions you need to obtain from work** (*refer to the grading of the benefits accruing from work that you completed in the questionnaire*)

**Preferred level of position**

**Preferred location(s)**

(*Are you prepared to relocate at all?*)

**Required minimum earnings package** (*package means basic salary plus any bonuses, commission or other earnings*)

**Required minimum guaranteed earnings** (*this normally applies to salespeople, or others whose income is made up of basic salary and other earnings*)

**Characteristics of preferred employer**

**Skills that you would like to be able to use**

**Skills that you would like to acquire**

You must now give some thought to the kinds of work that are likely to match this profile most closely.

This is, of course, more easily said than done, because you cannot hope to know all of the kinds of work that fit your profile – so you must endeavour to find out. Once again, professional help is one way to do this, but we are engaged here in a self-help exercise.

*Second Chances for Adults* is an excellent book that is likely to be available in the reference section of your local library. It lists an enormous variety of careers. Each section is written by a specialist in that field, and the information includes not only details of employers and training required, but also general remarks about the kind of work involved and the qualities needed to succeed. You should find information relating to the questions we ask in the Personal Profile exercise.

If *Second Chances for Adults* is not at your library, they will have something similar. Describe to the Librarian what it is that you are looking for.

These guides are probably most often used by people wanting to know the details of a career that they already have in mind, but you can also read through the individual entries to find those that appear to match the profile that you have designed for yourself.

# CHAPTER 5

## *How am I placed?*

The preceding chapters are likely to have thrown up possibilities for change. What you now have to decide is whether you can afford to make those changes – and that decision requires an appraisal of your financial position.

Draw up a personal Balance Sheet. This is a statement of your financial position. It deals with what you own (your assets) and what you owe (your liabilities), and a simple one might look like this:

| LIABILITIES | | | ASSETS | |
|---|---|---|---|---|
| Mortgage | | £72,000 | House | £215,000 |
| H.P. | | £7,000 | Spouse's car | £3,000 |
| Credit cards | £800 | | Savings accounts | £7,000 |
| | £1,200 | | | |
| | £900 | £2,900 | | |
| Overdraft | | £1,100 | | |
| Totals | | £83,000 | | £225,000 |

This Balance Sheet does not balance – the two sides have different values – and Balance Sheets are, after all, supposed to balance. That is where the name comes from. Having listed your assets and liabilities, you must now subtract one side from the other. The difference between what you own and what you owe is your net worth. In this case, it is the difference between £225,000 and £83,000, which is £142,000. So, we complete the Balance Sheet like this:

| LIABILITIES | | | ASSETS | |
|---|---|---|---|---|
| Mortgage | | £72,000 | House | £215,000 |
| H.P. | | £7,000 | Spouse's car | £3,000 |
| Credit cards | £800 | | Savings accounts | £7,000 |
| | £1,200 | | | |
| | £900 | £2,900 | | |
| Overdraft | | £1,100 | | |
| Net worth | | £142,000 | | |
| Totals | | £225,000 | | £225,000 |

The Balance Sheet gives no value for what may well be someone's biggest asset – their pension fund. Why do we miss it out? Because you cannot spend it. This Balance Sheet, remember, is designed to help you decide whether or not you are in financial shape for any change you might have it in mind to make in the way you live.

To prepare your own Balance Sheet, answer the Financial Self-Analysis Questionnaire, and then complete the Personal Balance Sheet Form we have provided. When you have done this, use the Income and Outgoing figures to prepare a cash flow forecast.

## PERSONAL BALANCE SHEET

| LIABILITIES | | ASSETS | |
|---|---|---|---|
| Mortage(s) | | House | |
| Bank loans | | Other real estate | |
| Overdraft | | Unit/Investment trusts | |
| | | Car(s) | |
| Other loans | | Savings accounts | |
| Credit card debts | | Current accounts | |
| Other debts | | PEPs | |
| | | TESSAs | |
| | | Government securities | |
| | | Quoted shares | |
| | | Other assets | |
| Net worth | _____ | | _____ |
| TOTAL | _____ | | _____ |

# FINANCIAL SELF-ANALYSIS QUESTIONNAIRE

NOTE: This questionnaire is designed to help you make decisions on how your future career is to be planned. It is not an investment aid, and it excludes many of the sort of questions that, for example, an insurance broker or investment planner would ask.

*Enter the following values as accurately as you can.* Do not fool yourself by entering exaggerated asset values – a house, for example, is worth what you can sell it for in the conditions prevailing at the time you bring it to market.

Before completing the questionnaire, read the notes which follow it.

ASSETS

    Your house
    Any other real estate you own
    Any car(s) you own
    Building society, bank and other savings accounts
    Bank current accounts
    Unit trusts
    Investment trusts
    PEPs
    TESSAs
    Quoted shares
    Unquoted shares with a ready market
    Government securities
    Loans made which can be readily realised
    Sums due from reliable sources
    Any other readily realisable investments

LIABILITIES

    Mortage(s)
    Bank loans
    Other loans
    Hire purchase agreements
    Credit card debts
    Other debts

Interest (*per month/ quarter/ half year*)
Dividends (*with due dates*)
Other income due (*with due dates*)

OUTGOINGS

*Monthly*

Mortgage
Monthly insurance
Pension plan
Loan interest
Housekeeping expenses
Hire purchase payments
Community Charge

*Non-monthly* (*with due dates*)

Insurance
Fuel
Telephone
Water rates
Other outgoings

## Notes on completion of financial questionnaire

You will notice that we ask you, when valuing your shareholdings, to include only those that are readily saleable. Quoted shares and Government securities can, of course, be sold easily; but you may have shares in private companies that would prove much more difficult to turn into cash. They still form part of your Net Worth, but you should not take them into account when considering a career move that may demand that you be able to turn your assets quickly into cash. Similarly, any loans you have made may or may not be quickly realisable, and you should value them accordingly. If you have investments in PEPs (Personal Equity Plans), you should examine very carefully the conditions under which they can be turned into cash before including them in a Balance Sheet of this nature.

Having completed the questionnaire, you are now able to draw up a Personal Balance Sheet and a Cash Flow Forecast.

In our example, we put the Net Worth on the Liabilities side, which means that your Assets are greater than your Liabilities. If you find that your figure must go on the other side, your Liabilities are greater than your Assets – you have a negative Net Worth, and less room to manoeuvre.

# PERSONAL CASH FLOW FORECAST

| | MONTH 1 | MONTH 2 | MONTH 3 | MONTH 4 | MONTH 5 | MONTH 6 | MONTH 7 | MONTH 8 | MONTH 9 | MONTH 10 | ETC |
|---|---|---|---|---|---|---|---|---|---|---|---|
| Income (A) | | | | | | | | | | | |
| Mortage<br>Housekeeping<br>Community Charge<br>Lighting<br>Telephone<br>Heating<br>Insurance<br>Pension<br>Other expenses | | | | | | | | | | | |
| Total Expenses (B) | | | | | | | | | | | |
| Optional Expenses (C) | | | | | | | | | | | |
| Surplus or shortfall<br>(A-[B+C]) | | | | | | | | | | | |

The Cash Flow Forecast is a vital tool that allows you to assess how well your projected income matches with your outgoings. Unless you have sufficient capital to allow you to meet your unavoidable outgoings from dividends and interest, you have to generate an income. There is no choice. Financial stresses are, in fact, one of the worst aspects of redundancy.

Your bank balance can look extremely healthy on your first day of liberty. The following day, it begins to fall. If you have been earning £35,000 p.a., it may take you six months to find a job. For the £50,000 p.a. person, that can be a year or more. Look back at the outgoings on your Cash Flow Forecast. You will not be able to avoid most of them. There is a very important question to be faced. How long can you last?

Some people, on losing their job, take any reasonable opportunity they can find, in order to generate an income while they go on looking for the job they really want. Do that if you really have to; but remember that you will have to explain your reasons at future job interviews, and that the interviewer is likely to form a modest view of your loyalty, your commitment, and – possibly – your common sense. The short term consideration may cost you your long term satisfaction.

There may be hard and unpalatable decisions that seem forced upon you. You have been earning £50,000 p.a. Your house is worth £220,000, but you owe £100,000 on the mortgage. You would not regard yourself as a spendthrift, but credit card bills amount to £4,800 and you have an overdraft of £3,200. Your net settlement on leaving your last company amounted to £14,000, which takes care of the debts and leaves you with £6,000 in the bank. The payments on that mortgage are £1,000 per month, your pension plan and insurance contributions are another £550 per month, Community Charge is £80 per month, and the monthly housekeeping absorbs another £350. Those outgoings alone are going to exhaust your cash reserves in just over three months; and it may well take you – at your income level – twelve months to find suitable work. You are the main breadwinner; your husband or wife is not producing enough income to make a hole in your expenses.

Of course, your bank manager knows that you are out of work, but knows also that you have considerable equity in your home, and is likely to be helpful with overdraft facilities. Overdraft interest is *high*.

There is an alternative. Sell the house, buy another, smaller, one with a much lower mortgage, and you are financially secure and free of worry for a lot longer.

Now, this is not a nice thing to think about. Your family loves this house, and so do you. Also, what will be the effect on the regard your friends and neighbours have for you when they see you selling up and getting rid of half your furniture? You will not want to do it, and perhaps

36

you will not have to. All we want to do is to encourage you to think the unthinkable. Look at all the alternatives. And how will you feel if you are still out of work this time next year, you then have to sell the house, and the equity has to go to clear your overdraft?

Of course, you don't want to sell the house. Neither, we suggest, do you want to add to the stress of being out of work the stress of being short of money. Did you know that financial problems are the single largest cause of marital breakdown in Britain today?

In any case, the decisions belong with you and your spouse. All we want to do here is to concentrate your mind on them.

When you are examining your financial position, you may be reassured by the knowledge that many of your commitments – Pension Plan contributions, mortgage payments, insurance premiums, even credit card debts – are protected by a provision that payments will be made on your behalf if you are redundant. Check them carefully. The fact is that many of these companies provide protection only for compulsory redundancy; people accepting voluntary redundancy are not covered. Yet, many people who have accepted voluntary redundancy will tell you that there was really nothing "voluntary" about it. This happens, for example, when you are offered the choice between accepting "voluntary" redundancy, or taking up another job in a place, or under conditions, that are not acceptable to you.

Let us look now at the implications of your Balance Sheet and Cash Flow Forecast for the viability of any career change you may be contemplating.

It may be that the way of life you are planning to take up provides an income greater than you already enjoy. Fine. If you are now able to meet all your commitments, that happy state of affairs will clearly continue. If, though, you are going to take a cut in income, you will have to assess whether or not you will be able to manage. This question has two parts:

• Will your after-tax income still cover at least your minimum outgoings?
• If not, is there any way to reduce those outgoings?

That last point should lead on to this: how many people are dependent on you? And should they be? Are you responsible for people who ought, in fact, to be standing on their own feet?

**Other factors.** Your state of health will influence how you should handle the rest of your life. Just how healthy are you? How much stress can you handle? And how much uncertainty? This is particularly important when you are planning to go into business on your own account, but think realistically about the hours you will need to work and about the stresses that the new line of work may impose. Are you fit enough to handle them?

Finally, a reminder that one of the benefits that work brings is that it provides a structure to the day and to your life. If you are thinking about a change, is the occupation you are considering one that will continue to provide this framework? If not, can you live happily without it? Or provide your own?

# CHAPTER 6

# *Finding a job*

Most jobs come from one of the following sources:

- Networking;
- Advertisements in the Press;
- The DE Job Centre;
- Speculative approach by the candidate; *and*
- Headhunters and Recruitment Consultants.

Remembering that this is a Career Development Book intended mainly for those in executive careers, we shall ignore the DE Job Centre as unlikely to have access to the kind of job you want.

## Networking

This is the name we now give to what used to be called 'The old-boy network'. The new term – dropping the sexist 'old-boy' – is preferred because the executive world is no longer a male preserve. Networking is about drawing on the web of people that you know, and on the people that they, in their turn, know.

The people you know are a valuable resource. Use them. Is someone you know already doing the kind of work that you want to do? Or someone who knows someone you know? Can they help you – with advice, with introductions, or with coaching? Do not be afraid to ask; this is no time for false pride. People like to be asked to help.

Make a list of all the people you have worked with. Against their names, record who they are now working for.

Treat the approach with some gentleness. Many people do not ask for a job, but rather: 'Do you know anyone who might be able to offer me a job?' If the answer is, 'Yes; my company'; so much the better. Or, try this: 'I'm going to be out of work at the end of next month. If you hear of anyone who might have a job for me, give me a call.'

One common approach is to contact someone who already works for a company you wish to target, and to ask her or him to get you an application form. This is wrong, for two reasons. The first is that you do not know how well your contact is viewed within that company. And the second, more important, reason is that application forms go to the Personnel Manager. As we will be discussing in the Topic on speculative approach to companies, the Personnel department is the wrong one to be approaching.

Do your networking early. If possible, start asking for help as soon as you know that you are going to be redundant, and before you are actually on the street.

## Advertisements in the Press

This is one of the major source of jobs – probably responsible for almost 20% of middle-ranking executive jobs.

Different newspapers carry different kinds of job ads – get to know where your kind of job appears. The only way to do that is to buy the papers. All of the papers, local and national. You will soon learn which ones you need to check regularly, and on which days they have the largest selection of jobs (Thursday is first for most national newspapers, followed by Wednesday.)

Go back to the Personal Profile you prepared. Have it by you when you go through the newspaper, and mark every advertisement that comes close to meeting your profile. In this respect, the most important considerations are:

- Type of work;
- Level of position;
- Locality; *and*
- Earnings package.

Age limits and qualifications are, surprisingly, less important, and you should not be inhibited from applying for jobs that you believe you can do but for which you are – at least according to the advertisement – too old; for which you do not have – according to the advertisement – a necessary degree or other qualification, or jobs for which you are at present – according to the advertisement – underpaid (that is, where the advertisement uses some such formula as 'applicants presently earning less than £x are unlikely to be suitably experienced for this position').

It may seem foolhardy to apply for jobs for which the terms of the advertisement seem to rule you out; but it is not. Of course, many employers will question your ability to read the simplest instructions, and many more will ignore you because they had prepared their profile for this position very carefully and knew precisely what they were looking for, but it is a sad fact that the majority of potential employers do not give enough thought to the kind of person they want to hire and your cv may focus their minds and make them realise that you are exactly what they wanted.

Most job advertisements, even where the company is named, are placed by recruitment consultants. You may imagine that our remarks in earlier paragraphs do not apply here, because consultants will have done a better job of preparing the profile, but to think this is perhaps to overestimate the abilities and qualities of consultants. In any case, drawing yourself to a consultant's attention is something we will be exhorting you to do in the relevant chapter.

Applying for advertised jobs is an art, and an art which most people fail to master. Getting it right can dramatically affect your success rate in winning interviews.

Job advertisements can get huge responses. It is now commonplace to hear of 700 people replying to ads. in the *Western Mail*, with the National Sundays getting even higher numbers. No one is going to read 700 applications. To get an interview, you have to make sure that yours is one of the applications that is read. And it is your covering letter, not your cv, that has to do that for you.

Let us take that company which received 700 replies to its advertisement. If yours was one of those, it would be nice to believe that they are going to read every single one. Nice – but naive. They aren't.

What is likely to happen is that they will decide how many people they want to shortlist for interview. Let us say that the number is six. Then, they will read precisely the number of applications that they have to read in order to get those six shortlisted candidates. Let us assume that they shortlist one candidate for every ten applications they read.

So they read sixty applications. Out of seven hundred. And what happens to the remaining six hundred and forty applications? They go in the bin. I'm sorry, but they do.

*You can enjoy considerable success in having your letter picked out, and read, instead of going in the bin, if you follow the advice given here.*

The first skill you have to learn is that of picking out the key words and phrases from the advertisement, so that you can draft your letter to highlight those areas where you meet their requirements.

Figure 6.1 is an example to help you plan your response to advertisements. Draft your own reply – start by picking out the key words.

**Engineering Manager**

**Plant Hire**

**c.£28,000, car**

**Yorkshire**

Subsidiary of a major plc specialising in the hire of construction equipment to Local Authorities and large building companies.

Rapid expansion and continuing capital investment creates need for professional to manage all aspects of equipment acceptance and maintenance.

Controlling a staff of six engineers, together with secretarial and admin. staff, the Engineering Manager will need as a high priority to review existing skill levels and procedures, to analyse training needs and to maintain strict budgetary control.

Candidates should ideally be Chartered Engineers, although other relevant qualifications may be considered, with a number of years experience in the acceptance and maintenance of heavy earth-moving and contracting equipment.

**FIG 6.1:** *Sample Advertisement*

The key words in Figure 6.1 are: *manage all aspects of equipment acceptance and maintenance; Controlling a staff of six engineers, together with secretarial and admin. staff; review existing skill levels and procedures; analyse training needs; maintain strict budgetary control; Chartered Engineers, although other relevant qualifications may be considered; a number of years experience in the acceptance and maintenance of heavy earth-moving and contracting equipment.*

Having picked out the key words, you write an application letter that is designed to show how you match up against them. Like this:

Your ref. xx/xxx

Dear Mr xxxxx

### ENGINEERING MANAGER

I refer to your advertisement in the Daily x of (date). As you will see from the enclosed cv, I am a Chartered Engineer with several years experience in the maintenance of heavy equipment, with considerable exposure to hydraulic systems and track-layers.

I am an experienced manager, both of engineers and of general staff, and I have run my department as a cost centre with full budget responsibility.

My management duties included identifying training needs and sourcing the solutions, from both internal and external trainers.

My experience and qualifications seem ideally suited to this opportunity, and I shall look forward to meeting you to discuss it further.

Yours sincerely


C. Engineer

**FIG 6.2:** *Reply to advertisement in Fig. 6.1*

---

You see what we did? We picked out of the advertisement those things that showed what the advertiser was really looking for, and then we showed how we met those requirements.

You won't, of course, have everything the advertiser is looking for. Don't draw attention to the fact. Don't say, 'Unfortunately I am not...', or 'Unfortunately, I have not...' Leave the advertiser to notice what you don't have. Remember – the exact person the advertiser wants may not exist, or may not be prepared to work for that company.

Salespeople know that people do not buy features – they buy benefits. An example of this from the salesperson's viewpoint would be automatic transmission on a car. This is a feature – but the good car salesperson will translate it into benefits, such as ease of operation in city traffic, smooth driving, good acceleration, which car buyers will recognise as desirable, and which will make them want to reach for their cheque books.

Follow the salesperson's example by picking out those things in your career which are features – your educational qualifications, your experience – and showing how they are likely to translate into benefits for an employer selecting you to do the job to be done.

Do not rehash your cv in the letter. The cv tells them what they need to know about you and your career – don't say it all again.

Be enthusiastic.

We gave above an example of a letter replying to a job advertisement. Here are some more.

*The advertisement was for a National Sales Manager with a well-known company selling production facilities on a job-by-job basis. Salary indicators were £30,000 basic; £60,000 OTE (On Target Earnings). Key words and phrases in the ad. were 'entrepreneurial'; 'graduate calibre'; 'track record of success in a progressive organisation'; 'flexible self-starter'; 'high level of energy'; 'skills and enthusiasm to motivate a successful team'; 'highly competitive market'; 'fast pace'.*

*One of the new Sales Manager's first objectives was said to be, 'to recruit and motivate a small sales team'.*

*The following letter assumes that the advertiser meant what he said (not always a wise assumption) and seeks to respond to these indicators.*

Your ref. xx/xxx

xx/xx/xx (Date)

Dear Mr xxxxx

### NATIONAL SALES MANAGER

I refer to your advertisement in today's 'Sunday x' and enclose my cv.

As you will see, my skills lie very much in the recruitment and management of new sales teams, and I have piloted no fewer than three companies from start-up to market leading positions in very competitive, fast-moving environments.

I attribute this success to my combination of sales and sales management skills with a commercially oriented business career that has equipped me to analyse and take advantage of opportunities before they have been fully identified by the competition.

Having taken my present company from nowhere to market leadership in three years, I now seek new opportunities to deploy these entrepreneurial skills, and am particularly interested in openings – such as the one you have advertised today – where my enthusiasm, energy levels and appetite for a challenge can bring rewards both to myself, to my sales team, and to my company.

I shall look forward to meeting you to discuss this exciting opportunity further.

Yours sincerely

A. Candidate

**FIG 6.3:** *Sample Application Letter*

*A 'major plc' was advertising for a Managing Director for one of its subsidiaries, described as a well-established, traditional furniture producer and supplier of trims to the motor trade employing approx. 300 staff.*

*Key words were 'Responsible for the day to day direction of the business'; 'maximisation of profitable future growth'; 'strong financial management, communication, logistic and organisational skills'; 'qualified, preferably to degree level'; 'Marketing or Technical background'; 'a knowledge of the trade would be an advantage'.*

*Salary indicators were £28-£35K.*

Your ref. xx/xxx

xx/xx/xx (date)

Dear Mr xxxx

### MANAGING DIRECTOR

I refer to your advertisement in today's 'Sunday x' and enclose my cv.

As you will see, I have been responsible for all aspects of running a substantial profit centre. In this position, I acquired strong financial and budgetary skills, and I conceived and carried through a reorganisation which resulted in productivity gains of up to 12%.

My technical abilities will be clear from the qualifications listed in my cv, and from my membership of relevant professional bodies, while my marketing skills have been honed by my involvement in the exploitation of new opportunities which has enabled my department to increase profitable revenue in high-margin product areas.

Before being promoted to this position, I was responsible for logistical tasks such as ensuring an uninterrupted flow of parts and components to the production facility, and establishing an efficient and cost-effective means of meeting customers' orders and urgent requirements.

I believe that I am now ready to take overall control of a 300-man operation, and I shall look forward to meeting you to discuss this opportunity further.

Yours sincerely

A. Candidate

**FIG 6.4:** *Sample application letter*

Here are some errors which many people make. Avoid them.

- Don't say, 'I enclose my cv for your attention'. Why else would you send it – so that it can be ignored?
- Don't say, 'I wish to apply for this job'. You are writing; the job is mentioned in the heading of your letter; you are sending your cv. Is it really likely that you would be writing to say, 'I just thought I'd let you know that there is no way on this earth that I would apply for your job'?
- Don't say that you are available for interview at their convenience. If they want to see you, you will hear. Don't grovel.

Everything we have talked about to this point is designed to get you the interview, once the letter is read. But we have said that most letters are *not* read. It is, of course, the appearance of your letter that will get it off the pile and into the advertiser's hand.

Unless your handwriting is immaculate, or the advertisement specifies handwritten applications, type your application letter, preferably on the same paper as your cv is typed on. Keep the letter short – never more than a single A4 sheet. Refer to the job advertised and say where you saw the advertisement, quoting the date of the publication. Make the letter as business-like as possible.

Do not skimp on paper quality. The correct size to use is A4, which is 210mm x 297mm. This is the size used in business for business letters. The colour should normally be white, although our remarks about coloured paper for cvs also apply here. Coloured paper may sometimes be acceptable; white is always safe (though some people may see it as boring). Paper quality is measured at least partly by its weight, in grams per square metre, written $g/m^2$. You should find the weight on the end of the packet or box. $70g/m^2$ is photocopier paper, and too thin. Do not use it. The minimum acceptable weight for this purpose is $80g/m^2$, and $100g/m^2$ is best.

The question of typing can be a vexed one. If you are out of work, you may have left your typing facilities behind you. It is also true that some employers prefer a handwritten letter – but they are in the minority, and, in any case, how good is your handwriting? Some employers use graphologists to draw inferences about a candidate's suitability and psychology from his writing. Do you want your descenders and flourishes to be more important in deciding your suitability for interview than your qualifications and experience?

In any case, the appearance of your application is terribly important. At the time of writing (May 1991), advertisements in the *Sunday Times* for jobs paying salaries of £35,000 p.a. or more have been known to attract between 1,000 and 2,000 applications. Your application has to stand out. It is all that you have to represent you.

So, if you do not have your own typing facilities, do your best to get some. Ask your old secretary, or your partner's secretary; ask a neighbour; or look up secretarial agencies in the Yellow Pages.

Or perhaps you could buy a wordprocessor or typewriter? It may pay, in the long run – from the figures we have just quoted about the volume of responses to job advertisements, it will be clear that you may have to send out an awful lot before you are finally placed.

## Speculative approach by the candidate

Writing letters to companies you would like to work for has always been a job-hunting method with a high success rate. There are two reasons for this; one is that speculative applicants save the cost of advertising and the trouble of sifting applications and interviewing many people, and the other is that, by writing, you demonstrate a strong interest in the company.

To score with a speculative letter, the quality must stand out. Have it typed on a good typewriter with an attractive typeface, and use good quality paper – see our remarks about application letters in response to advertisements.

How many speculative letters should you send out? A lot. The figures we quoted earlier for typical numbers of replies to job advertisements will have pointed up for you the competitive nature of today's job market. Speculative letters may take away some of the competition, because you are applying for jobs that have not yet been advertised, and whose existence is therefore not yet widely known, but:

- you will not be the only person sending a speculative letter to those companies
  *and*
- many of the companies you write to will not be able to use you.

Increase your chances, therefore, by writing to as many companies as seem appropriate. If only one company in a hundred can use you, you know how many letters you need to send out, don't you? Ninety-nine will be just one too few to be sure of success.

In fact, we suggest that you send out your letters in batches of twenty per week, for at least ten weeks.

You can't find that many? Yes, you can.

Begin with a trip to your local reference library. They have there two reference books that will help you enormously. One is *Kompass*, and the other is *Kelly's Directory*. They are also likely to have locally produced directories.

*Kompass* comes in a number of volumes, and you want the one that gives company information. For England, you begin by turning to the section that deals with the county you want to work in, and then look up the towns that appeal to you. Entries for Wales and Scotland are divided by town only. The information given will vary by company, but the minimum will be:

- Company name;
- Address;
- Telephone number;
- Number of employees; *and*
- Product codes.

The product code tells you the kind of business the company is in, and you can find the key elsewhere in *Kompass*, with a more detailed breakdown in another volume. Ask the reference librarian – they have a wealth of expertise which they are rarely asked to use, and will be delighted to help you.

Many companies have more detailed entries, which may provide some or all of the following information:

- How to get there;
- Annual turnover;
- Name of parent company;
- More detailed description of their business; *and*
- Names of key directors and managers.

We recommend that you be cautious over the names given – they are frequently out of date. Always telephone to check the name of the person you want to write to, even if it seems to be given in *Kompass*.

Other sources of company names are the local press (news of companies just starting up in business usually appears there first); Yellow Pages; and your friends.

In addition, look at the job advertisements in the Press. Where the job advertised is in the wrong field, or at the wrong level, to fit your profile, but where the other factors do fit, write them a speculative letter instead of a reply to the advertisement. However you find them, get your speculative letters out there in the large numbers we have recommended. Job-hunting is a full-time occupation.

The choice of person to write to is critical. You need to approach the person at the head of the department you want to work for. So, if you are an engineer, write to the Works Director, Works Manager, or Technical Director. Accountants should write to the Financial Director or Chief Accountant; and so on. Only write to the Personnel Manager if the Personnel Manager is the person you want to work for.

There are as many possible wordings as there are companies to write to, people writing and jobs that they are writing about. What we can do is to present an example and some guidelines. Here are the guidelines:

Write to a person, not a job title. Decide who you want to contact –
Managing Director, Personnel Manager, Financial Director, Marketing
Manager, whatever is appropriate – and telephone the company and
ask the switchboard operator the name of that person, so that you
can write to her or him personally.

Say, 'I wonder if you would mind giving me the name of your (say) Manufacturing Director?' When you have got the name, say, 'And is that
his (her) title? Manufacturing Director?' You do this because, if the
company does not have someone with precisely the title you have
asked for, the switchboard operator will often give you the name of
the person who most closely matches the one you have asked for.

Do not be afraid to call back. If you are asked why you want to know,
explain, but do not be put off by being told that they have no vacancies. The telephonist does not run the company, and does not know
who or what is wanted. Do not, however, be rude.

If asked whether you want to speak to the person, say no – politely –
write down the name and go back to your letter. It will sometimes
happen that you telephone and ask for someone's name, only to
hear 'One moment, please', and to find that you are being put
through. Hang up. You are not ready for this conversation.

You will sometimes run up against a company whose policy is not to
give out names over the telephone. This is usually for security reasons,
and will typically happen with defence companies, food manufacturers,
or companies whose political situation may be delicate. If the company is a large one, chances are it produces published statements,
and the names of the directors – security or no security – are likely to be given there. All you have to do is drive up to reception, or
telephone the Company Secretary's department, and ask for one.

Alternatively, do you know anyone who works for, or with, the company?
Can s/he help?

If these methods get you nowhere, ask for the Managing Director's
secretary and explain to her why you want to know.

Only if you draw a blank in all of these ways should you write to 'The
Managing Director' and address the letter 'Dear Sir'. The imper-
sonal nature of this approach will reduce the letter's impact – you
don't even know whether the Managing Director is a man, and yet
writing to 'Dear Sir or Madam' is probably even worse.

When a letter is written to a person, you end it 'Yours sincerely'. If
you cannot find out the name and have to write to a job title, end
the letter 'Yours faithfully'.

If you are doing your own typing, remember to leave two spaces after a full stop and one after a comma.

Make your letter enthusiastic. You cannot be there when it is read, so only the letter can show what a truly wonderful person you are.

Do not put your life story in the letter. Enclose a cv, and keep the letter itself short.

Do, however, mention one or two outstanding points about your background, and relate them to the company's likely needs – remember our earlier remarks about selling benefits, not features.

If you know, make it clear what kind of job you are asking for.

Do not say that you will telephone to arrange an appointment. This used to work, but people are so tired of it now that it has become counter productive.

---

Here are some sample speculative letters:

Mrs xxxxx
Managing Director
Target Company plc
22 Bull Street
Outer Circle
Anytown AN2 6GH

xx xx xx (date)

Dear Mrs xxxxx

I enclose my cv. As you will see, my experience over the past five years has embraced all aspects of planning, specifying and installing computerised production control facilities within large factories. Running my department as an autonomous profit centre, I have also gained considerable understanding of the commercial realities that control such an operation in the nineties, and I am skilled at recruiting and motivating staff.

Target Company plc seems to me to be a company that might well offer me the opportunity to deploy these skills in the context of a new challenge, and I shall hope for the opportunity to meet you to discuss any such openings that you may have.

Yours sincerely


A. Candidate

**FIG 6.5:** *Sample speculative letter*

Dear Ms ........

The challenges I was set over the past five years have now come to an end with the takeover of my company by Walters and Co plc. As the enclosed cv will reveal, I have developed first class skills in FMCG marketing, and I now need the opportunity to use these skills in a demanding, fast-moving environment.

Your reputation is for providing just such an environment. Can we meet to discuss what we can offer each other?

Yours sincerely



Martin Attridge

FIG 6.6: *Sample speculative letter*

---

Dear Mr ........

I wonder whether we could meet?

My six years in private practice have given me the skills and experience detailed in the enclosed cv.

I am now seeking the logical next move; and I believe that this may well be offered by the new distribution subsidiary that, I understand, you are to set up.

I shall telephone you over the next few days to see whether we can arrange a suitable appointment.

Yours sincerely



Jane Bolam

FIG 6.7: *Sample speculative letter*

Note that these are examples, not standard letters for you to copy. If you are one of many people following this course at the same time, you do not want local companies getting the same letter from lots of different people. The object is to show how special you are – not to raise a smile on the Personnel Manager's face.

Now here are some guidelines on how *not* to write a speculative letter:

• Don't ask a friend who works there to get you an application form. Application forms go to the Personnel department, and we have already told you the drawbacks to that.

• Don't (oh, yes, we have seen it done) begin your letter: 'Are you looking for a good man (woman)?' The answer may be, 'Yes, but not in the way you mean'.

• Don't say that you think you are the person the company is looking for (how can you know?), or that you believe you can do a great job for the company. Be enthusiastic, but don't put it like that.

• Don't go over the top. Distinguish between enthusiasm and exaggeration.

• Don't say that you are available for interview as required. They know that. Say that you *look forward to* an interview.

• Don't mention the salary you earn now, or how much you are looking for.

---

## Headhunters and recruitment consultants

Headhunters and Recruitment Consultants exist to bring job-hunters and employers together.

They get their fee from the employer, not the person employed. It is based on the salary and other income of the person placed, and it follows that they have a very clear incentive to put people into jobs. If they fail to place you, they earn no fee for you, and that is what you represent to them – a potential fee. Agencies can do an excellent job for you, but this fundamental truth is one you would be wise never to lose sight of.

You will find local agencies in the Yellow Pages, and you should register with them. To do so you will have to submit a cv or fill out the agency's own form (you may have to do both), after which you will be interviewed. This interview is different from a job interview, but there will be similarities. The interviewer is not deciding whether to take you on, but what sort of employer to send you to. You are not deciding whether to work for the interviewer, but trying to convey what it is you want to do.

It is easy to feel very positive after a meeting with a consultant, and this feeling is often misplaced. Good consultants will be concerned with a number of things, and these will include your welfare. They will not regard you as a perishable commodity, and will not be thinking primarily of the need to get you placed, and a fee invoiced, before someone else does. If they really believe, as experienced professionals, that your ambitions are unrealistic, they will say so. They will not try to talk you out of doing the things you really want to do and into doing the things they have vacancies for, merely to earn a fee at your expense. When they have clearly understood what you want to do, they will search their records for a suitable vacancy. If none exists, they will approach possible employers on your behalf, but only after discussing them with you.

That is what good consultants are like. Most agents and consultants will try to get you to take the jobs currently on their books. They will discourage you from following your own desires if your own desires do not match available vacancies. They will send out your cv on a 'scatter-gun' approach, without so much as a word in your direction. They are also likely to tell you that they have been retained to fill a vacancy when the truth is only that they happen to know that the vacancy exists – perhaps it has actually been assigned to one of their competitors – and they will then pass your details to the company in the hope of getting you taken on.

They will also be enormously enthusiastic when talking to you, and you will leave their office convinced that a good offer will be on its way to you within days. This is a nice feeling, but a dangerous one – because their enthusiasm will almost always be assumed. If you allow yourself to be buoyed up, you will soon face depression; and when you have been through that cycle a few times, you will begin to lose confidence in yourself. And that is bad. What you must do, therefore, is to work with the consultant but remain sceptical until you see evidence that the rosy prospects held out to you are genuine.

Headhunters cultivate mystique about what they do. The basic difference between them and recruitment consultants is that consultants advertise jobs they are retained to fill, while headhunters know who will best fill the role, or at least know how to find that person, and will approach the candidate directly.

In fact, there is considerable overlap. Headhunters do not always know where the candidate is to be found, and consultants often approach directly people they already know. Many firms, in fact, undertake both types of assignment.

It is unwise to wait until a headhunter tracks you down. Give him/her a helping hand by letting him/her know where you are, what you can do, and what you are looking for. Here is a sample of the sort of letter you should write to consultants and headhunters.

Mrs A Consultant
Executive Placement Firm
People House
Any Street
Anytown XX1 1YY

*Date*


Dear Mrs Consultant

I am currently Marketing Manager at Miraculous Solutions Ltd, having joined the company when it was set up five years ago.

Having been responsible to a considerable degree for the company's success – we are now the largest player in this market, with twenty-two percent market share – I now find myself urgently in need of new challenges.

I enclose my cv from which you will see that my forte is the exploitation of short windows of opportunity in fast-moving, high tech products. I also have considerable experience of work with European distributors.

My preference would be to work with a smaller company, and the minimum package would be of the order of £52,000.

Should you be retained to fill a vacancy for which my background fits me, I shall look forward to discussing it with you.

Yours sincerely


A. Candidate

**FIG 6.8**: *Sample letter to recruitment consultant*


Send out as many of these speculative letters to headhunters and recruitment consultants as you can. First, though, you have to know who and where they are. One way to find out is to look at advertisements for the kind of jobs you want, and write to the consultants who placed them. This method, though, will only locate a small fraction of the available firms for you; so you will need to bolster it by checking reference books.

There are two that deal with this subject. One is *The Executive Grapevine*, published each year by the company of the same name whose address is: 79 Manor Way, Blackheath, London SE3 9XG. The other is *The CEPEC Recruitment Guide*, from CEPEC Publications, Kent House, 41 East Street, Bromley, Kent BR1 1QQ.

Write and ask for a copy – they are not cheap, but are worth it.

As each of these manuals lists hundreds of consultants, you will be unable to write to each one. Some are, in any case, highly specialised – there are consultants who only recruit lawyers; others who deal with accountants; and some working only in, say, the chemical or engineering industries. Each will have an entry that gives not only the industries they work for, but also shows the percentage of their placements both in each of several job functions and in each of several salary ranges. If you are looking for a Divisional Manager's position at £50,000 p.a., you are unlikely to be successful with a firm that places seventy-five percent of its candidates in sales and marketing jobs with only five per cent of them making more than £35,000.

The entry will also tell you who to send a speculative letter to. Do not be put off if it says that speculative letters are not accepted – that is for the benefit of clients, not you. You represent a fee on legs to any consultant you deal with, and they are not going to turn down someone for whom they have a place.

After you write your letters, you should get a reply from all of them – a dramatic difference from the situation with letters to companies, and replies to advertisements.

You will also receive phone calls from any who think they might have immediate openings for you. All consultants ought to interview you before sending you to see a client. Many, unfortunately, do not take their job this seriously.

# CHAPTER 7

# CVs – How to tell your life story

CV is short for *Curriculum Vitae*, a Latin term meaning, for practical purposes, life history. In fact, of course, what is required is the story not of your life but of your career.

We frequently hear this from job-seekers: 'As soon as I saw the advertisement, I knew the job was for me. Every qualification they wanted, I had; all the experience I was looking for was on my cv. I didn't even get an interview. I don't understand it.'

Well, we understand it. There are two reasons for this common experience. The first (which we mentioned when talking about job ads) is that the cv was never even read. The second is that the cv was read, but was not good enough to win an interview – not good enough, in other words, to do its job.

A cv is a selling document. It is there to sell you. Finding a new job is, under present conditions, both challenging and demanding; your cv will make it easier or it will make it harder. The cv will usually be the only thing that the consultant or prospective employer knows about you. If s/he has advertised a single job and received two hundred and fifty replies, the interviews will go to those whose cvs stand out. You must make sure that this includes yours. If you don't get an interview, how on earth are you to get a job?

There are two aspects of the cv that will attract, or repel, the reader: the content, and the form. We are going to deal with content in some detail. Before we do so, let us talk about form.

First, paper. For safety, use white, A4 size, and good quality. Paper weight is described in grams per square metre – $g/m^2$ – and is marked on the end of the box. $100g/m^2$ is best, but never use less than $80g/m^2$.

White, we said, was for *safety*. There are industries – advertising springs to mind – where other colours may be acceptable, or more than acceptable; and there is certainly a theory that a cv on coloured paper will stand out in the pile on the prospective employer's (or consultant's) desk. It remains true that you cannot offend with white; and that you may do so with any other colour.

Some people bind their cvs. We are against this practice, because it makes you look like a professional job-hunter. Of course, the prospective employer knows that you are looking at many employers; but you should write your cv as though it was addressed only to her or him.

A cv *must* be typed. If you cannot do that yourself, you must make arrangements to have it done. A neat, well laid out, well typed cv will go a long way towards getting you an interview. If you do use a typewriter, make it a good one. A microcomputer with word processing software is best, but be sure to use a printer with real letter quality output. This means a daisy-wheel or laser printer, or one of the really good dot matrix printers that have a 24-wire print head and produce real letter quality output. It does *not* mean an ordinary dot matrix printer that allows you to see the dots that make up the characters. If you have the equipment to handle it, justify the text – which means, have even margins right and left, just like a book.

CVs are not about responsibilities and lists of jobs; they are about achievements. That is one of the most important statements in this book – so important that I shall repeat it. **CVs are not about responsibilities and lists of jobs; they are about achievements**. We hear endless arguments about typing or handwriting; about paper colour; about format. All of these arguments have weight, but they are all utterly sterile when compared with the argument about history v. achievements.

What is the potential employer likely to buy? *Not* the fact that you were responsible for the accounts of a group, or supervised seven people, or ran a company, or maintained a factory's electrical systems. No; the potential employer reads about your achievements, and thinks: 'If s/he did that for X Company, *s/he could do it for me.*' It is statements like this that excite employers:

> • I developed a new test rig which reduced testing time by 30% and extended the operating life of the machinery by 25%;
> • I pioneered a new method of consolidating accounts which provided information 3 days earlier each month and which was subsequently adopted throughout the Group;
> • I rationalised the operations of a group of service engineers so that the additional 15% of service calls were handled with no increase in the number of engineers and with no deterioration in response times. This provided a 12% over-performance against budget.

Note the form of these statements. In each case, they begin with a description of what the person did – *I developed a new test rig* – and follow it with a summary of what that meant to the company – *reduced testing time by 30% and extended the operating life of the machinery by 25%.*

This is the magical formula which enables employers to say, 'If s/he did that for *them*, s/he could do it for *me*.' And it is that promised benefit to the employer that elicits the job offer.

Salespeople know that people do not buy features – they buy benefits. Job titles and responsibilities are features. Achievements are benefits. The job of your cv is to present benefits that the person buying you will enjoy. Those benefits will be described through your achievements.

You don't have achievements to talk about? Yes, you *do*. We have never met anyone who could not describe achievements – once they understood how to look for them. So, let us talk about that.

'That wasn't an achievement. That was just doing my job.' Fine. It was still an achievement. You are there to achieve. Because salespeople know that people buy benefits, not features, they learn to apply the "so what test":

FEATURE: AUTOMATIC BRAKING
'This car has ABS, which is a set of microprocessors and circuitry attached to the brakes and wheels.'
'So what?'
'So you can stop on a wet bend without skidding.'
Therefore people buy the benefit of safety.

FEATURE: FAX MEMORY AND AUTO-DIALLING
'This fax machine has a large memory, and the ability to re-dial engaged lines automatically.'
'So what?'
'So your operator only has to pass the document through once. If the line is engaged, the machine automatically stores the content of the fax, and retries the number again and again until it gets through – although your operator is now doing some other job for you.'
Therefore people buy the benefit of efficiency – the reduced time taken by fax operator.

Does that make features and benefits clear? In a cv, achievements – benefits – will almost always be described in terms of greater productive time, reduced costs, greater throughput, jobs done in less time, higher sales, greater efficiency – and this is either translated into percentage terms or expressed as a sum of money.

Find your achievements by asking these questions:
• Why does/did your employer have you there, doing that job? What did s/he expect to get out of employing you?
• What would have been the result of *not* having you there?
• What would have happened if you had got it wrong?

Next, put yourself back into the body of the person you were when you were doing each job. Someone said something good about something you had done. It might have been your boss, a colleague, a subordinate, or a customer. What was it that you were congratulated on?

This task of finding your achievements is one of the most important you will have. Work at it.

Now, content. There are many ways to write a cv, and they all have their adherents. We cannot possibly deal with all of them, and so we are going to begin by putting together a cv that follows one well used and successful format – one that is likely to be acceptable in most circumstances. After that, we will discuss one of the alternative approaches.

Let us make this point, however. *No single model of cv can possibly be suitable for everyone.*

Take the simple question of age. Regrettable though it may be, many employers do discriminate on grounds of age. If you are over, say, forty-five, putting that fact on the first page of your cv may be a mistake. The employer is conscious of your age throughout the time she or he reads your cv, and so reads it in a negative frame of mind. If your age appears on the final page, s/he will first become aware of your achievements and abilities, and it may be that your age will then have a less damaging impact. They have been impressed by your experience and there is, after all, only one way to get experience. So, people over the age of 45 may decide to put their "house-keeping" details on the last, instead of the first, page.

Make sure, though, that you do give your name, address and telephone number on the first page. You may like to lay it out in the same way as we have done for Mary Baines (see page 65).

Again, how about Profiles? When you look at the cv for Mary Baines, you will see that we have used a Profile on Page 1 to describe her. Some people always put a Profile on a cv – but it is not always right to do so. If the person's qualifications and experience are not particularly impressive – as may be the case with a younger person, for example – a Profile will make this clearer. Do not be a slave to fashion.

In the model that we have used for Dave Fisher, the first page provides a brief summary of who and what you are, and should enable the reader to find you when he wants you. Refer again to our remarks above, to decide how much of this information should appear on your first, and how much on your last, page.

You must give your name, address and telephone number. Don't rely on the recipient keeping the covering letter and the cv together – especially if the cv is going to a consultant – make sure that anyone can find you just by reading the cv.

Your date of birth is also essential.

Educational details come next. Show the highest qualifications you have, and the place where you got them. If you have a BSc from Birmingham, it is not necessary to show the subjects in which you got eight 'O' Levels at Tamworth Grammar; but if those are all you have, detail them.

Important courses you have attended can also be shown. The difference between 'educational details' and 'courses' is sometimes difficult to pinpoint. Briefly, courses will include work-related topics like Health & Safety at Work, and any craft skills such as welding. They will also include courses – whether taken internally or externally – on management topics, and on such things as computer skills, including the ability to use a computer programme. On this last subject, we recommend that you name any 'proprietary' package that you can use – this means software that is generally on sale, like Lotus 1-2-3, Microsoft Word, Aldus Pagemaker, Autocad and so on. Such skills can make you highly saleable. If you are skilled at a programme that was written by or for your company, and is only used by them, it is no use referring to it by name, since that name is unlikely to mean anything to someone from outside your company. Instead, say something like, 'I am skilled at data entry and the use of *xyz Company*'s Database software'.

Also name any foreign languages you speak. This means that you are reasonably proficient in those languages, and can do more than simply ask for two beers in a local bar. It is not necessary to have a formal qualification – indeed, many people with an 'O' or 'A' Level in a foreign language would be ill-advised to claim proficiency as a linguist.

Most people mention leisure interests and, as long as mention them is all you do, it can do no harm and might be thought to present a fuller picture of you. The drawback can be that readers feel that you cannot have time for the hobbies you quote and still work as hard as they expect at your career. Note that we say, 'leisure interests', and not hobbies, because the range that you can cover is wide. If you are, or have been, on a committee, a school governor, or the coach of a children's sports team, that says a lot about you. Put it down.

Other topics that are often mentioned in cvs are Marital Status, Driving Licence, State of Health, and Referees. We recommend that you do not include the last two of these, and that you mention Marital Status only if it enhances the picture of stability which a cv aims to present.

Those remarks apart, Page 1 of your cv on the Dave Fisher model will look like this:

# Curriculum Vitae

DAVID ALAN FISHER

| | | |
|---|---|---|
| Address: | 31 Marsh Place | Tel.: 0101-10101 |
| | Anytown | |
| | Anyshire | |
| | AN10 8AT | |

| | |
|---|---|
| Date of Birth: | 27th February 1943 |

| | |
|---|---|
| Marital Status: | Married, 2 children |

| | |
|---|---|
| Education: | Birmingham University |
| | – B.Sc. in Electrical Engineering |
| | 4 x 'A' Levels |
| | 11 x 'O' Levels |

| | |
|---|---|
| Courses taken: | PERA course on Computers in Machine Shop Scheduling |

| | |
|---|---|
| Professional Memberships: | A.I.E.I.Eng |

| | |
|---|---|
| Languages: | French, German |

---

You are not finished with Page 1 yet; you should show a Career Summary at the foot. You may find that it takes quite some time to get all the dates right. Take the trouble to do it properly. Note that you should start with the most recent and work backward.

That is almost the end of Page 1. You will notice that we have not mentioned salary. Views differ on whether salary should be shown in a cv; our recommendation is as follows. When preparing a cv to send to a recruitment consultant or headhunter, put in your desired salary or total earnings package.

When sending a cv to a potential employer, leave salary out. Thus, Dave Fisher's cv, amended for submission to a Headhunter, would look like this:

# Curriculum Vitae

DAVID ALAN FISHER

| | | |
|---|---|---|
| Address: | 31 Marsh Place | Tel.: 0101-10101 |
| | Anytown | |
| | Anyshire | |
| | AN10 8AT | |

Date of Birth:         27th February 1943

Marital Status:       Married, 2 children

Education:            Birmingham University
                            – B.Sc. in Electrical Engineering
                            4 x 'A' Levels
                            11 x 'O' Levels

Courses taken:        PERA course on Computers in Machine
                            Shop Scheduling

Professional Memberships:    A.I.E.I.Eng

Languages:            French, German

Salary Indicator: £52,000 p.a.

Employment Summary
    1986 to present Works Director, French Ltd.
    1980 to 1986     Parrish and McKechnie, ending as Production Controller
    1974 to 1980     Works Manager, Central Water Authority
    1964 to 1974     Various functions within Smith and Bamboo Ltd

---

Long cvs are boring, and people stop reading before they get half way. A cv should last no more than three pages, and we have used one for the summary. This leaves only two pages to deal in detail with the rest of your career. This is good, because lack of space means that you are going to have to work hard at condensing your accomplishments into few words, and doing that will force you to examine what exactly it is that you have to say about yourself.

Pages 2 and 3 describe your career history to date. Here, you give the highlights of the various jobs you have done, with particular emphasis on what you achieved while doing them. List the jobs in the same order as in the summary on page 1 – starting with the most recent and ending with the first. This order is chosen because a potential employer is most interested in what you have been doing recently.

The following, based on the cv developed in the two preceding figures, is a sample of the way these sections are written. **Note the stress on achievements**.

---

## Career History to date

<u>1986 to present.</u> I joined French Ltd. as Works Director, and have held that position for 4 years. During that time, the scale of the operation has grown as follows:

Output in value terms: £13 million to £24 million (85% growth)

No. of factories: 2 to 4 (100% growth)

Manufacturing employees: 1200 to 1900 (58% growth)

In addition to managing this impressive growth, I have been personally responsible for the equipping of the two new factories, recruitment of a new and skilled workforce, and the selection, specification and implementation of computerised manufacturing control in a company that had no such capability before my arrival.

Having brought the new plants and systems into satisfactory operation, I now seek the stimulation of new challenges elsewhere.

---

This is an example of what we have discussed before – presenting achievements in such a way that the potential employer says: 'If s/he did that for them, s/he could do it for me.' It is an example of selling benefits, not features.

You must select from your career those aspects – achievements, elements of experience, etc. – that are going to make a prospective employer notice you. Remember why you are writing a cv. You are doing it to attract attention. You are doing it to make yourself stand out in the job-hunting crowd. You are doing it to excite the reader.

Boring prose does not excite. Yards of print do not attract. Job descriptions do not stand out.

What you have to do is to analyse your performance in each job very carefully, and pick out those things that you did well. You must also identify the skills and experience that each job gave you. Then – briefly, but giving everything its correct weight – you must put those achievements and that experience into words that will ring true to the reader. And remember that people who read cvs regularly become awfully cynical.

There is a theory that cv's should always be written in the third person – saying 's/he' instead of 'I'. This has become as outmoded as ending letters 'your obedient servant'. If a consultant is submitting your cv for you, the consultant will of course refer to you as 's/he'. But for your own cv, 'I' is the expression most commonly used today. Note that we say 'most commonly used'; writing cvs in the first person is now usual, but the third person remains an option for those who prefer it.

Accept that you are going to have to re-write the cv again and again. You will have one version to send with speculative letters to recruitment consultants. You will have another to go with speculative letters to potential employers. This may well be the same cv as the one you normally send in reply to job advertisements; but never reply to an advertisement without picking out the key words, as we mentioned in Chapter 6. Measure yourself against these, and then ask whether the standard cv needs to be modified to bring out some particular point that this advertiser seems to be looking for. Job hunting is not easy. Following our advice should put you at least some way in front of the competition.

## Other approaches to cvs

We said that the cv we have just put together was one, successful, general purpose model. There are other ways of approaching the task.

A common one is to turn the approach on its head, and to put personal details like age, address and so forth on the final page. In this model, these details are merely the "housekeeping" items, and the first two pages are used for what is seen as the more important tasks of describing the kind and level of job sought, and to provide a personal profile of the job-seeker.

Here are some examples of profiles. Note that the profile *can be* – it is a question of personal choice – the one place in the cv where we use the third, rather than the first, person.

---

### SAMPLE PROFILE FOR FACTORY MANAGER

Accomplished Factory Manager with excellent communications skills. Has experience of developing and controlling a multi-disciplined workforce within the process industry. Successfully maintained and developed good communications within the organisation, while controlling a budget of £1.5 million.

---

## SAMPLE PROFILE FOR MECHANICAL SUPERVISOR

Extensive experience within a highly technical production system. Skilled organisational abilities have enabled him to co-ordinate manpower and materials to achieve production targets. Career to date has included making a significant contribution to the development of production processes together with full appreciation of the importance of developing good communications and teamwork.

## SAMPLE PROFILE FOR ACCOUNTING OFFICER

Accomplished in the areas of corporate finance and accountancy. Current position at *XYZ Co. Ltd* has been reached by clear and continuous progression through the industry. Excellent organisational and inter-personal skills together with a sound appreciation of the need to develop good communications and teamwork. Adaptable and versatile approach to the requirements of any new work. Seeks an opportunity to deploy present skills and experience, and to contribute to her new company's success.

## SAMPLE PROFILE FOR SURVEYOR

A fully qualified and highly competent Chartered Mineral Surveyor. Skills and experience can easily be translated into other areas of surveying, especially where the highest standards of professionalism and accuracy are essential. Experienced in the design and planning of new development, and in co-ordinating the efforts of engineers, planners, solicitors and other professionals. Competent in the negotiation and preparation of planning applications. Aware of environmental needs as factors tempering commercial reality.

On the following pages we reproduce a cv written along these lines, for Mary Baines.

36 Garfield Place
Anytown
Anyshire
ZZ1 1ZZ

Telephone: 0000 – 00000

## MARY BAINES M.Sc. MBA

POSITION SOUGHT

A post that will offer new challenges in Market Research, Planning and Advertising, preferably in FMCG, providing opportunities both to bring on junior staff through training and supervision and to contribute to the solving of complex product marketing problems through marketing audit skills and through the coordination of various marketing disciplines and of both internal and bought-in resources.

PROFILE

A marketing professional of long standing who has the ability to relate to people at all levels and to coordinate successfully the exponents – both in-house and external – of many marketing disciplines. With a proven track record in developing and bringing to market complex FMCG products, and establishing them as leaders in highly competitive markets, I am hard-working, committed and imaginative, and am aware of the degree to which sensitive management, by drawing out of people the best they have to offer, can contribute to corporate success.

My particular abilities are to:
DESIGN AND SPECIFY new products in the light of Market Research data.
BRING THESE PRODUCTS TO LAUNCH POINT by coordinating design, pricing and manufacturing efforts.
ANALYSE reasons for success and failure of products, and success and failure of marketing campaigns.
DEVELOP, with the aid of outside specialists, integrated marketing campaigns and to monitor these for success.

**Page 1 of Mary Baines' CV**

## SELECTED ACHIEVEMENTS

NEW PRODUCT INNOVATION
Developed several new FMCG products including toothpaste, washing powder and soaps from first product specification to initial launch, including post-launch audit.

ADVERTISING CAMPAIGNS
Analysed the rates and causes of success and/or failure of previous marketing campaigns. Drew up plans and objectives for new marketing campaigns, agreed them with senior management and briefed external agencies. Monitored the work done by external agencies to ensure that the brief was adhered to. Supervised the choice of advertising media to ensure maximum coverage commensurate with the approved budget.

PLANNING AND ANALYSIS
Conducted Market Research to examine the depth and quality of public perceptions of the company and its products. Drew up, and agreed with senior management, marketing plans to obtain the best possible recovery from approved budgets.

**Page 2 of Mary Baines' CV**

---

The remaining pages would then give the career history, very much as we have already shown and arranged from the most recent to the oldest, with the final page giving details of age, marital status, education, training and any other points that Mary Baines wanted to bring out.

## Good English

When you have written your cv, we would like you to do something you will find hard – we would like you to write it again. Treat your first draft *as* a draft. Very few people can write really well first time. Like any good writing, a well presented, easy to read cv is the product of hard work, and much rewriting. Here are some rules to help make sure that your English is at least as good as it should be.

- Use short words and sentences rather than long.
- Use simple, straightforward words, where possible, and Anglo-Saxon rather than Latin or Greek words (see below for more on this).
- Use the active rather than the passive voice – say, for example, 'I was responsible for', and not 'my responsibilities included'; 'revenue grew by 50%', not 'there was a 50% growth in revenue'; and 'I commissioned and installed new systems', rather than 'new systems were commissioned and installed'.

- Apply the speech test – have you written as you would have spoken? If not, your written English is probably too stilted.
- Read through what you have written, and cut out every single word that can conceivably go without changing the meaning. Isn't there a more compact way of saying what you have said? Don't be twee, humorous or pompous.
- Check the meaning again. Have you really said what you meant to say?

On the subject of simple language, writer and grammarian Harold Herd wrote an excellent guide to good writing called *Watch your English*, in which he says, 'If you would write plainly, beware of affected words and phrases. Do not write *eventuate* when you mean *happen, conversed* for *talked, demise* for *death, a member of the stronger sex* for *man, organ of vision* for *eye, voiced the opinion* for *said*.

If Herd were writing today, he would be warning against usages like *utilise* for *use*, and *purchase* for *buy*. To summarise, a cv is the most important weapon in the job-seeker's arsenal. Without a good one, you will not get to see the consultant, or prospective employer, that you need to see. So take your time – a good cv can take a week to put together.

Accept that you are going to have to re-write the cv again and again. You will have one version to send with speculative letters to recruitment consultants. You will have another to go with speculative letters to potential employers. This may well be the same cv as the one you normally send in reply to job advertisements, but never reply to an advertisement without picking out the key words, as we showed in Chapter 6. Measure yourself against these, and then ask whether the standard cv needs to be modified to bring out some particular point that this advertiser seems to be looking for. Job hunting is not easy. Following our advice should put you at least some way ahead of the competition.

Here is a practical example. To make it as realistic as possible, we have taken a real advertisement – the candidate is not, of course, a real person. It will help us achieve two aims: to illustrate this point about adjusting the cv to the advertisement's key words; and to show you a complete cv, on which we can then make comments.

An advertisement for a Personnel Manager included the following key words and phrases: *to develop a forward thinking, effective and innovative contribution to the business; a mature individual; make a strong contribution in a fast moving and intellectually challenging business culture; ambitious resourcing programme; provide effective people solutions; experience of employee communications programmes, and handling grievance and disciplinary matters; a full knowledge of UK employment legislation, with understanding of EC employment regulations and initiatives; first degree level intellect; in your thirties or early forties; experience in at least two businesses; work independently and as part of a management team.*

The applicant, Mr I.L. Persons, responds to these key words and phrases with the following claims:

He has a BA and both parts of his Institute of Personnel Management exams.

He has several years experience in recruiting, handling grievance procedures, and developing employee communications programmes, as well as leading a personnel department.

He is accustomed to working in a fast-moving environment.

He is used to developing, as well as implementing, strategies.

The following figures show how Mr Persons' cv will look.

# Curriculum Vitae

**I L PERSONS BA MIPM**

10 Parkside
Burton on Trent
Staffs
DE5 3XX

Tel: 000 0000

Date of Birth:  3rd May, 1949

**Profile**
An ambitious individual who combines a degree-level education with extensive personnel experience and qualifications. Intelligent and quick-thinking, he rapidly reaches the heart of a problem, and is at his best when entrusted with establishing personnel policies and carrying them out. Performs at his best where the workload is both varied and challenging.

Presently responsible for personnel in a £40 million business employing 600 people at three sites. Through a staff of four, administers all aspects of training, personal development, union negotiation, rewards management and conception and implementation of human resource strategy.

His excellent communication skills make for credibility throughout the organisation.

Education:   BA Upper Second in English (Durham University)
             Institute of Personnel Management, Parts 1 and 2

Professional Memberships:   Corporate Member, Institute of Personnel Management

Employment summary:
1970 to present Alpha Manufacturing Company
   1987 to present   Personnel Manager
   1985 to 1987      Assistant Personnel Manager
   1981 to 1985      Industrial Relations Officer
   1977 to 1981      Recruitment Officer
   1972 to 1977      Manpower Officer
   1970 to 1972      Graduate Trainee

Leisure Interests:   Chess, swimming, photography

Other achievements: Was secretary of PTA for five years

Courses:   CEPEC counselling skills course
           Alpha Manufacturing's Management programme

## Career to Date

Alpha Manufacturing is a group of companies turning over £40 million p.a., and operating almost entirely within the High Tech industries. One of the tensions this creates within a personnel department is that the rate of technological change demands constant attention to training to avoid high staff turnover and to enable the companies to compete successfully in their markets.

I joined Alpha on their 'fast track' graduate intake programme, and selected personnel early because of an emerging realisation of the degree to which corporate problems can be overcome by proper attention to 'people' problems. Noting a failure to keep staff aware of developments within this fast moving industry, I developed a communications programme using in-house magazines, newsletters and videos recorded by senior management – which has been identified as a major factor in keeping morale high and turnover in staff to a minimum. As Recruitment Officer, I pioneered the use within Alpha of sophisticated psychometric and other testing methods, and established an Assessment Centre. This has reduced by 50% the number of staff lost within 3 months of recruitment, with a saving to the Group of more than £300,000 p.a. With union agreement, I negotiated a grievance procedure which has cut the number of days lost through strike action by 30% – reducing lost turnover by more than £2 million p.a.

For the past four years, I have been in overall charge of the personnel function throughout the group. In this role, I am an integral part of the senior management team, and am proud of the contribution my department has made to meeting the organisation's overall commercial objectives while maintaining an essentially human face to operations.

I now seek further challenges in an organisation which will offer me the opportunity to add to my skills, knowledge and understanding of people; and to use these personal enhancements to improve the competitive position of the organisation for which I work. I seek to be part of an organisation which values people, and looks for competitive edge through them.

**Page 2 of I.L. Persons' cv**

Several aspects of this cv will be instructive. I.L. Persons has written: *For the past four years, I have been in overall charge of the personnel function throughout the group.* When he first wrote this sentence, it read: *For the past four years, my responsibilities included overall charge of the personnel function throughout the group.* Reading it through, he realised that he had used the passive voice – and changed it.

At the end of his description of his present job, I.L. Persons gives his reason for wishing to change jobs. He makes this statement a positive one

– a desire for new challenges – even if it is really no such thing. It is never a good idea to malign a present or past employer in a cv. It is, on the other hand, acceptable to say that a takeover or restructuring has curtailed opportunities that were there in the past.

He concentrates on statements of achievement, and makes those achievements ones that are likely to commend him to the person for whom the cv is written. Doing this has enabled him to focus on some of the key words and phrases picked out from the advertisement.

Note, finally, that I.L. Persons does not meet every requirement of the advertiser. In particular, he has not got experience of two businesses – he has worked for Alpha since leaving University. *He does not draw attention to this shortcoming.*

Townsend, the management writer and one-time Chief Executive of Avis, says that if someone has 50% of what a job requires, they can grow into the rest. That may be a little ambitious for some people – those who are already fulfilling all of the potential that they have – but it is certainly true that many job applicants who cannot offer the experience and knowledge that the employer requires will nevertheless make a good fist of the job – if they can get it. The cv has to help them overcome what they lack.

That is not to say that you should lie in a cv. If you do, you are likely to be caught out. What you can do is to write the cv in such a way as to maximise your claims and minimise those areas where you fall short.

We end this chapter with a summary of what we have learned here.

---

### CV PREPARATION – REMINDER OF MAJOR POINTS

• Your cv must represent you, because you will not be there. Make it stand out – in appearance and in content.

• Job-hunting in the nineties is a full-time occupation. You cannot afford to have one cv for all purposes. Extract the key words from the advertisement and tailor your cv to meet them.

• Long cvs are boring. Keep yours as short as it can be, while still saying everything that must be said.

• Follow the tips in this chapter on writing good English.

• You must not lie; but you can use all of the resources of the infinitely expressive English language to help you present things as you wish.

• Write in the first person.

• Only quote salary expectations on a *speculative* cv to a recruitment consultant.

• Achievements are what make someone want to hire you – so achievements are what you must write about. Blow your trumpet.

• Radiate enthusiasm.

• Write a draft. Read it carefully. Rewrite it. Write it again. Don't lose an interview because you could not be bothered to take enough pains. Pain is a lot of what job-hunting is about.

## CHAPTER 8

# *Going for it – How to excel in interviews*

Job interviews are difficult for most people, because most people are not salespeople, yet you are there to sell – yourself.

Consider this question. If, tomorrow, you were due to take – say – an 'A' Level exam in Physics, and if someone offered to show you the paper in advance, you would be likely to accept the offer. Then, you would go away and prepare yourself to answer the questions on the paper.

Well, an interview is like an exam in which you already know the questions – or most of them – because the same lines of questioning come up again and again. And yet, so few people bother to prepare properly. Follow the advice we give here, and you will be way ahead of the competition.

Something else we would like you to remember about interviews is that the interviewer *wants* you to succeed. S/he has a problem, and the solution to that problem is a person. If you turn out to be that person, the interviewer can forget about the problem and get on with her or his job.

The first thing that any competent salesperson does before even attempting to make an appointment is to research the target company. And so must you. Always research a company before attending an interview. It flatters the interviewer, and it shows that you have initiative.

What sort of research should you do? Well, you need answers to these questions:

- (For manufacturing companies) What do they make?
- (For service companies) What service do they provide?
- (For distribution companies) What do they sell?
- Who do they sell it to?
- (Roughly) How big are they – in sales, and in employee numbers?
- Are they growing?
- How long have they been in business?
- Who owns them?
- Who do they compete with?
- What do people think of them?
- What is it that makes people buy their products?

These are the minimum of things you need to know. Why? In order to impress the interviewer, and thus improve your chances in the competition you will undoubtedly face for the job; and also to satisfy yourself that you really do want to work there. If you are applying for some types of jobs – in sales, accountancy or marketing, for example – you will want to know more.

There is other information that is useful to have if you can get it – and the recruitment consultant who sends you for interview is the most likely source. How does this interviewer interview? What turns her or him off? Does she or he have a standard approach, or pet questions?

So now we know what you need to find out – but how do you do it?

How do you actually research a company?

First, there are the reference books, like *Kompass* and *Kelly's Directory*. Go to your local reference library and look them up. While you are there, ask about any directories of local companies, or directories covering the kind of company – engineering, for example – to which you are applying.

Then, is the company a plc, or a subsidiary of a plc? (Getting the answer to the first question is easy – the initials 'plc' will be in the company name. To find out whether your target is the subsidiary of a plc, check the directory *Who Owns Whom* in your local reference library. Having a stock exchange listing imposes certain obligations on a company, and one of these is of use to you. A plc must produce an annual report, and must send a copy to anyone who asks for it. So, telephone the Company Secretary's department of the company you are applying to, and ask for one.

The annual report will contain a lot of information, some of which will only be really useful to you if you are an accountant. For most people, the most valuable section will be the Chairman's Report. Here, the Chairman tells shareholders about his company, its results over the past year, its plans for the future, what factories it is opening or closing, what products it is launching or discontinuing, how it is dealing with competition and many other things.

This information will be enormously useful to you at interview – provided that you use it to plan what you are going to say. Suppose, for example, that you learn from the annual report that the company plans to open a new factory in the next year or so. Then, to the question, 'Where do you want to be in three years time?', you could answer, 'I know that you are expanding, and opening a new factory in ....... I believe that that kind of growth is likely to mean real opportunities for everyone in the company.'

Again, suppose that the annual report tells you that the part of the company to which you have applied is in the business of making high performance parts for specialised sports cars. To the question, 'Why do you want to work here?', you could answer, 'I know that you make high performance parts for specialised cars. That sounds like a very satisfying business to be in, and I would like to take up a challenge like that.'

Another form of research is very simple – telephone, and ask for information. You don't have to keep your reasons secret – they won't think you are spying! Companies *like* candidates to research them.

Or, try going along there and asking the receptionist – or the sales department – for some sales literature.

Other people are also a source of information:

- People who work there;
- People who sell to them;
- People who buy from them; *and/or*
- People who compete with them.

Suppose, for example, that you are applying for a job with a supermarket chain. After talking to people who shop there, you could answer the question, 'Why do you want to work here?' by saying, 'I know that you concentrate on giving people a good deal by stocking relatively few lines, and charging very competitive prices. That sort of service to the public appeals to me.' Or, when asked whether you have any questions, you could say, 'I know that you recently launched a range of low-priced products in your own packaging. How has it gone? Do you plan to extend it to other kinds of product?'

If you ask a customer of the company that is interviewing you why he buys their equipment, he may say, 'We have bought from them for some years, because their service is excellent. But their products are getting long in the tooth, and we'll have to switch suppliers if they don't come up with a new range soon.' Now, your answer to the question, 'Why do you want to work here?" would be, 'Because you have such an excellent reputation for service.' When asked for your own questions, you would say, 'Your products are very good, but they are being left behind. Do you plan a new range?'

When you have done the research, you will be in a position to undertake the interview. We are now in salesperson's territory – and salesperson's rules apply.

Rule number one is to be on time – and that means early. Remember the salesperson's old adage; if you are not five minutes early, you are late. Check out in advance where the interview is to be held. If you do not know the area, drive or walk by in advance of the interview so that you know where to go. If you are travelling by bus, make sure you know which is the correct bus route, and the time of the last bus you can catch to get there on time.

And ensure that the location you are checking out really is the one where you are going to be interviewed.

Rule number two is to be smart. This means clothes appropriate to the kind of job you are seeking, and clean. Suit or jacket and skirt or trousers cleaned and pressed. Shirt or blouse clean and ironed. Tie clean. Shoes polished. Remember the second old salesperson's adage; you never get a second chance to make a first impression. The most important word in this paragraph, though, is appropriate. Dress as you believe a decision-maker for *this* company would expect an applicant for *this* job to dress.

If you have qualifications, take the certificates with you. If during your working life you have received letters of congratulation, confirmations of achievement, league tables in which you figure towards the top, take them with you. If you have references, or anything else that speaks well of you, take them with you. If you have ever been written up favourably in the Press for work-related reasons, take a copy with you. Make sure that all of these items are clean and well cared for. Do not allow them to get dog-eared. And have them easily accessible. Do not find yourself searching through an untidy briefcase, muttering, 'I know they're here somewhere', under the interviewer's raised eyebrow. Best of all, have a duplicate copy of your "good boy file", and leave it with the interviewer.

The interview starts just before you come in sight of the building. Do not be seen attending to your appearance. If you need to brush your hair, do it before you turn into the road. If you need to brush your shoes, do it before you turn into the road. If you need to clean your car, *you should have done it before you turned into the road.*

At reception, tell the receptionist who you are there to see, and then say, 'Before you tell him I am here, may I use the men's/ladies' lavatory?' This gives you the opportunity to check your appearance in the mirror, straighten your tie, wipe a smut from your face, and (for men) undo your trousers so that you can tuck your shirt neatly into them. (Remember to do them up again, or you may find yourself in the wrong sort of inter-view.)

You will be met at reception either by your interviewer, by a secretary, or by someone else. If it is your interviewer:

  • Smile and look her or him in the eye – hold eye contact.
  • Hold out your hand to shake hers or his.
  • At the same time, repeat your own name – as in, 'Hello, Mr Bloggs. I'm Jane Smith.'

These things help you make that vital first impression.

If it is anyone else, smile and make whatever polite conversation seems appropriate. Remember that the person taking you to meet your interview-er may very well pass on comments, favourable or otherwise. Make them favourable.

If you now meet the interviewer in his or her office:

- Smile and look her or him in the eye – hold eye contact.
- Hold out your hand to shake hers or his.
- At the same time, repeat your own name – as in, 'Hello, Mr Bloggs. I'm Jane Smith.'

In the interview room, do not:

- Sit down until you are asked to do so.
- Lean or rest on the interviewer's desk.
- Light a cigarette, even if asked to do so, and even if the interviewer smokes.

When you sit down, pause for a moment to relax. Breathe in deeply, let the breath out slowly, and concentrate on relaxing your muscles. Do not, however, flop. Hold yourself as though you have pride in yourself.

There are three things, not one, that the interviewer is trying to learn, although s/he may not be conscious of all of them. The first is whether you have the skills, abilities and experience that she or he is looking for; the second is whether you will fit easily into the existing team; and the third is how she or he would feel about having you around all day. Some interviewers are very good at this. Some are dreadful. Most are somewhere in between. Your job is to help them choose you – in salesperson's parlance again, to give them your own way.

You cannot do this by remaining mute. You have to tell the interviewer about yourself. You must not, though, appear to talk too much.

How do you manage this difficult balancing act? Well, how do sales people do it? By careful listening, by thinking about what they are hearing – and by asking questions. A good salesperson has been described as having two ears and one mouth – in that proportion. If you listen carefully, you will pick up lots of clues about what the interviewer really thinks and is really looking for. Feed them back, and show how you fit the interviewer's requirements.

If the interviewer is businesslike, this will be fairly easy. If the conversation rambles, you will have to grab it and put an end to the rambling. This means taking charge of the interview, and will be a lot easier if you have thought beforehand about the job, what it entails, and what sort of questions the interviewer should ask you. If you are not asked these, say something like 'I expect you would like to know about...' and then give your prepared answer.

One thing you simply *must* do is to ask what sort of person the interviewer is looking for. Do not respond immediately, but listen carefully to the answer, so that later you can carefully show how you meet each criterion. Most good salespeople do not sell products (although they may seem to do so); they sell solutions. Your interviewer has a problem – a need – why else are they looking for someone? You have to sell yourself not as a person – a product – but as the best available solution to the problem.

Many people are wary of asking this question, but those who do so soon realise how well it works. An interview is a conversation, but a special kind of conversation which you want to go in a particular direction. Questions *give* a conversation direction. But be sure to ask this one early. (The ideal time is right after the interviewer has described the job to you).

Do not ask about money, holidays, pension arrangements, or anything of that sort until the interviewer mentions them.

We cannot possibly know what lines of questions the interviewer is going to ask you. There are, however, both old chestnuts and common lines of questioning that are worth getting to know, so that you can be prepared for them if they do come up. We will deal with some in a moment. Before we do so, a word about answering technique. You are not in this interview to win arguments. You are not there to impress the interviewer with your extensive knowledge of the world scene. What are you there for? You are there to get a job. Nothing else. So when you are asked a question, do not ask yourself 'What answer will best allow me to show myself in a good light as against this interviewer?'; but 'What answer will be best calculated to make the interviewer see me as someone that they really should hire?'

Now, the questions we promised you.

**Why do you want to work for this company?** 'I need the money' is not an acceptable answer. You cannot answer this question unless you know something about the company, and that means that you need to have done that research we talked about.

Having done so, you know quite a lot about the company. This makes the answer to the question *Why do you want to work for this company?* fairly easy – but only if you have thought about it and rehearsed it before you go in. Pick out those things that suggest that this company will give you the ability to develop a career, or to fulfil your personal aspirations, or whatever else your research has suggested is realistic.

**Where do you want to be in three years time?** 'Sitting in your seat' is one of the commonest answers to this question. This is unfortunate, because it is the wrong answer. You have no reason to believe that the interviewer is yet ready to yield his or her seat – to you or to anyone else. What the right answer is will differ according to: the nature of the job you are applying for; the career structure of which it forms a part; your own aims; and so forth. If you are ambitious, it may be correct to say so here – and it may not. You must think it out in advance. Look back, though, to the answer we offered you when we were talking earlier about research. That answer was non-specific – it did not identify a particular ambition which the candidate wanted to satisfy. Since you don't usually know enough about the company to be specific in your ambitions, this is usually a good approach.

**What do you do in your spare time?** Answer briefly, and wait for a supplementary question before giving more information. Raising rare bulbs from seed, reading about the history of small Welsh railways or running up and down Scafell until you drop may be fascinating to you, but do not assume that the interviewer shares your interest. *Do not go on about it.* S/he will think you are a nut – and most companies are not looking to employ nuts.

**What do you believe this job entails?** is a question asked by good interviewers. It is looking for a specific answer rather than generalities. For example, the question, *What is the job of the High Tech salesperson?* should be answered like this: *The job of the High Tech salesperson is twofold. S/he is the entrepreneur who identifies the business opportunities available to his company, and s/he is the team leader who coordinates all of the resources of the company in order to turn those business opportunities into profitable revenue.* An answer like this shows that you have thought deeply about what it is that people like you actually do, and why companies employ you to do it. 'They form good relationships with people', does not. So, think about the nature of the job you are in; ask yourself, not, 'What do I do?' but 'Why do they have me here doing it?'; and plan your answer to this question.

**What would you say are your particular strengths?** is a question that ought to follow on naturally from the last one, but it is usually asked on its own. Being able to down twelve pints of beer before collapsing is probably not what the interviewer is looking for. The strengths at issue here are those which will make you a valuable acquisition for this company in the role they have in mind for you. This is a very common question, and you need to think about your answer before you go into the interview.

**What are your weaknesses?** This, fortunately, is less common, but it does come up often enough for preparation to be a good idea. The kind of weakness to confess to is the kind that shows you in a good light. Perhaps you might discover that you are sometimes impatient with colleagues who fail to treat deadlines with sufficient urgency? Or how about a suspicion that you are perhaps – just ever so slightly – too much of a perfectionist? Whatever you do, do not say that you have no faults at all. The interviewer may suggest some.

There are two answers to this question which are common but also wrong. The first is: 'I am a workaholic.' This is not a good thing to say, because it can produce either of two unfortunate responses in the interviewer. One is that a workaholic is someone who cannot get the work done in the time available. The other, which is equally undesirable, is: 'Oh, good. This candidate will work evenings and weekends whenever I ask.'

The second common wrong answer is: 'I don't suffer fools gladly.' Apart from suggesting that you are intolerant, these words carry a coded message in English. When someone says, 'I don't suffer fools gladly', s/he is often seen to be implying: 'And you are one.'

**What salary do you expect?** This is an unfair question, but that will not prevent it from being asked. A salesperson's ploy when price is mentioned too early is to say, 'I'm not dodging the issue, but I always feel that the first thing we have to do is to satisfy you that this is the product you want to buy, and that we are the people you want to deal with. When we have done that, I promise you, price will not be a problem.' If, therefore, it is still very early in the interview, say, 'I wonder if we could look at that when I have a clearer idea of what you are looking for and you know whether I am likely to fit the bill?' Then ask a question of your own, to move attention elsewhere.

When the question comes up later and the advertisement stated a salary range, say 'The advertisement mentioned £xx' – picking the top figure that was mentioned. Let the interviewer explain, if he or she can, why you should not command the maximum figure they are prepared to pay. If no money was mentioned but you know what similar companies pay for similar work, you should once again ask for a high, rather than a low, figure. You are less likely to lose the job through seeming to think highly of yourself than through self-abasement.

If you have no 'pay indicators', do not name a sum at all. Instead, turn the question back on the interviewer by saying something like, 'What *is* the salary range for this position?' Not many companies these days operate without job grading and a set of laid-down pay ranges for each range. The range may be a long one, though, and if the money they suggest is inadequate, you must say so.

And if you are forced to name a figure with nothing to guide you, name a substantial one. To the comment, 'You're expensive', reply, 'No, I'm not expensive. I cost a lot of money, but I'm not expensive.'

**How will your wife/husband feel about your being away a lot?** Don't say that the family realise that work comes first. The interviewer may share this view – and may not. If you are a man, you can talk about the solidity of your relationship and how your partner understands the calls made on you by work. Women can also use this reply, but should remember that it may be a "discriminatory" question – one that would be asked by that interviewer of a woman, but not of a man. Be on guard.

**What would you do if you disagreed with an instruction given to you by a superior?** Say that you would present your reasons for disagreeing, but that management's job is to manage, and that you would carry out any ethical order, once you had explained your objections. (If you have doubts about this, I invite you to contemplate how you would handle this little beauty:

> INTERVIEWER: Let me put this question to you. We, as you know, do a lot of business in the Middle East. Let us suppose that the Marketing Director comes to you and says, 'We have a chance to sign a contract for £3 million. Naturally, this being the Middle East, we are going to have to pay sweeteners – about 10% of the total.' He asks you, as Finance Director, to make the money available. What are you going to say?
> YOU: ???

**Why should you be the person who gets this job?** Don't criticise other candidates, and don't say that you are the best person for the job. You cannot know that. Restate the interviewer's criteria (the kind of person s/he is looking for), and show how you meet them.

**Tell me about yourself.** Begin by answering the question, but get your question – 'What sort of person are you looking for?' – in very quickly. Otherwise, you may be off at a tangent. You cannot sell a solution until you know what the problem is.

**What happens if you get married/you start a family/your husband is moved?** These questions are addressed to women, and are discriminatory. Don't start a fight, and don't take a confrontational approach, but stand up for yourself. You have no plans at present that would interfere with your ability to do a good job.

## "Odd" questions

Some interviewers – generally those who have read a paperback on psychology – specialise in asking questions which, they think, give them an insight into the candidate's psychology. Here are some.

**I want you to think of the person – male or female, in work or out of it – whom you most detest. Done that? Don't tell me the name. What is it about that person that you really dislike?** If you answer this – for example, by saying that the person you really detest is sly, devious and self-centred – the interviewer follows up with this: 'That's interesting. Did you know that psychological theory says that, when we really hate someone on that scale, it is because we recognise something in ourselves which is so repugnant to us that we cannot own it?' You are now in a trap, from which there is no way out. The only sensible answer (after a moment's thought) is: 'Detest? No. There are people I don't really care for, I suppose, but detest? No, I don't feel that strongly about anyone.'

**Think back over the past ten years. What have you done that you are most ashamed of?** Amazingly, people do answer this honestly. Don't. Say: 'Oh, I guess we've all done things we wouldn't do again. But I can't think of anything I'm deeply ashamed of. I think that level of regret is negative. Don't you?'

**What are your children called?** The interviewer almost certainly believes (and, if you think about it, so do you) that you can tell a lot about a person from the names they choose for their kids. The kind of person who asks this is probably not going to give a job to someone who chose, say, Elvis, or Shane. If your child is called Elvis Shane Smith, you have a problem.

On a wider point, do not give specific answers to questions until you are quite certain that you know enough about the company and the job to be certain that the specific answer is also the right answer. Keep the conversation general until you know.

Through all this, show enthusiasm – for the interviewer's company, the job and the prospect of working for him or her. Even if you decide during the interview that you do not want the job, go on acting as though you did – first, because every interview is good practise and second, because turning down a job you have been offered is much more fun than not being offered it in the first place.

Do not ramble. If you find yourself doing so, *ask a question*. That shuts you up, and gets the interviewer talking.

And remember that instinct plays a large part – far too large a part – in most people's hiring decisions. Many interviewers will tell you, 'You always know within the first three minutes'. Well, no one can know within the first three minutes of an interview whether the interviewee is the right person for their company to hire; but as instinct is given such a high priority, you had better play to it. Smile as often as you appropriately can – but make it the smile of an equal. Do not be obsequious. Look alert, and intelligent. Do not lounge, and do not rest your hands, your briefcase, or anything else on the interviewer's desk. And, once again, do not smoke.

Now, your own questions. The interviewer should ask at some point whether there is anything that you want to ask him/her. This is your opportunity to shine. However thoroughly s/he has described the job, it is a mistake to say 'no' unless you absolutely have to. You will look weak. To avoid this, you should have thought in depth about the company and the job before you attend the interview. If you have done so, questions will have occurred to you and you should now ask them. Once again, though, do not ask questions about money, holidays or other benefits until the interviewer opens this subject.

If your research has not thrown up questions to ask, try something like these:

- What are the most important skills you are looking for?
- Do you see increased responsibility coming to me in the future?
- How will my performance be measured?
- What is the company's attitude to training?

And, of course, the essential one: *Am I the kind of person you are looking for?*

If your research has suggested problems with this company – the possibility, for example, that it may be in financial difficulties – it is not out of order for you to raise the subject.

If the interviewer's description of job, company and benefits package has been so complete that you really do have nothing left to ask, respond to the request for questions by moving straight into what you must, anyway, do at the end of every interview, which is:

**Close**. This, once again, is salesperson's talk, and means: Ask for the order. Ask them for the job. Say something like: 'Am I the sort of person you are looking for?' If you took the precaution earlier (and you should have done, because we told you to) of getting the interviewers to specify what sort of person this was, now is the time to remind them of their wish list and show how you meet it. Conduct your conversation as though you are assuming that, of course, the job is yours.

Do not expect to close successfully the first time. You must expect to encounter what salespeople call 'objections' throughout the interview. An objection is something that casts doubt on what you are selling – in this case, yourself – or on what you say. It may be genuine, or it may be fake – in which case it almost certainly hides another, genuine, objection.

A typical objection encountered in an interview would be, 'You do not have sufficient experience in (say) overseeing a pool of mechanics.'

When you encounter an objection, your first job is to ensure that it is genuine. You do that by testing it. A simple way of testing the objection we have just given would be to ask, 'If I did have sufficient experience in that area, would you hire me?' You may wish to make this a little less blunt, but it does have this advantage: if the answer is, 'Yes', you know that the objection is genuine. You do have everything else he needs to offer you the job.

If, on the other hand, the answer is, 'No', then you know that your lack of experience in running a pool of mechanics is not the decisive factor in preventing you getting the job – and you need to find out what is. To do this – you ask!

Many people dislike the idea of asking for the job, worrying that they will seem too pushy. Please don't have this fear. Provided that you do not go over the top, the interviewer will not be offended – will, indeed, probably not even notice that you have asked. The important things to remember are:

• Stick to the style and substance that are comfortable for you;
• Modify your approach to fit the interviewer.

Early in 1991, we had a perfect example of the usefulness of this approach. A 25 year old woman who had been on a BCE self-marketing workshop went for an interview as secretary to a Director at one of the major banks. She felt that the interview went reasonably well but, when she asked, 'Am I the person you are looking for?', she received this answer: 'Well, we really do feel that you are a little too young to be able to do a job like this.' She dealt with that objection by going back over her previous career and showing that she could, indeed, accept the degree of responsibility involved in working as secretary to a bank Director.

The point is, of course, that she was only able to deal with the objection because she knew it existed, and she only knew it existed because she *asked*. Had she not done so, she would have had a good interview, but she would not have got the job.

Sometimes of course, you uncover an objection to which you have no answer. Fine. So you don't get the job. You weren't going to get it anyway. Wouldn't you rather know now? Again and again, people spend two weeks of hope after an interview, when the interviewer knew before they had left the building that they were not going to be successful.

Throughout a sales call, the salesperson checks for agreement. S/he is constantly asking, after making a point, questions such as: 'Does that make sense?'; 'Would you agree with that?'; and 'How do you feel about that?' Cultivate the same technique during interviews.

Through all this, never lose sight of your objective, which is: to be offered the job. Find out what interviewers think they want, and try to offer it to them. Remain on equal terms. Act in such a way as to make them see you as someone they will be happy to work with.

And *ask for the job*.

---

## INTERVIEW TECHNIQUE – SUMMARY

- Job interviews are *selling* interviews, and you are there to sell yourself.
- Research the company fully before you get there.
- If you are not five minutes early, *you are late*.
- Dress appropriately, and smartly.
- Make sure your car is clean, inside and out.
- When you meet the interviewer: smile; hold eye contact; say his or her name; introduce yourself.
- Do not sit down until asked to. Do not lean on the interviewer's desk. Do not smoke.
- Take control of the interview. Ask what the interviewer is looking for.
- Think out in advance the likely questions, and plan your answers.
- Plan questions of your own.
- *Ask for the job.*

# CHAPTER 9

# *Working for yourself*

In Chapter 3 we dealt with the personal qualities needed if you are to succeed in business for yourself, and we will not repeat that discussion here. How, though, do you go about it?

**Planning**. The well-known lecturer Chester Karrass said that a plan was like a road map: 'You can walk, drive or take a bus; but if you don't know where you want to go, you won't get there.' It doesn't matter whether you want to be a part-time window cleaner or set up a factory making cars and employing twenty thousand; you still need plans, and you need, surprisingly enough, the same plans. Those we will look at are: Mission Statement; Business Plan; Cash Flow Forecast.

**Mission Statement**. 'Mission Statement' is a very high-flown way of referring to a statement of what you intend to achieve. Do not let the 'high-flown-ness' put you off. Most people do work on the basis of 'how do I know what I think till I see what I say?', which is only to say that writing your thoughts down clarifies them. So, put your intention in writing. A mission statement should be brief, but it should also say everything that you want to say about what you plan to do. Do not go into the detail of how you are going to do it – that comes next.

Typical mission statements look like this:

- To be the largest office cleaning and janitorial supplies company in Anytown.
- To secure an income of £200 p.w. from car valeting.
- To raise from seed and sell by mail order sufficient rare bulbs to produce an income of £12,000 p.a.

Get the idea? Write your mission statement now.

**Business Plan**. The Business Plan comes after the Mission Statement. It cannot come before, because until you have completed your Mission Statement you do not know what to plan for. We write Business Plans for two reasons: to translate the Mission Statement into a blueprint for action, and to provide a document that will support an approach to a lender. To these, add one that is a hybrid between the two, and that is: to sell the business to yourself. You believe that you want to go into business in this way; the Business Plan ought to satisfy you that it is, or is not, a practical possibility.

Nor should you leave it there. After your business gets under way, check regularly that it is performing in line with the Business Plan, and take steps to correct any negative deviations.

You must begin by putting values on what you aim to do, and this may involve market research.

For example, if you do plan to be the largest office cleaning and janitorial supplies company in Anytown, do you know what this means in cash terms? How big is the company which presently holds this position?

Now, how do you plan to achieve your aim? If we take the example of the office cleaning and janitorial supplies company, they would want to work through the questions on page 96.

This is the time to introduce the concept of margin. Margin does not mean the same as 'mark-up', which is the percentage by which cost is increased to obtain selling price – so that, for example, something bought for £60 and sold for £120 is marked up by 100%; if it is sold at £180, it is marked up by 200%; if at £240, by 300%; and so on. While there may be a mark-up of 100%, or 200%, or even 1000%, there can never be a margin of 100%; margins might approach that figure but they can never reach it. If it costs us £100 to produce or buy in a product and we sell it for £200 we have marked up the price by 100%, but we have a gross margin of only 50%. To arrive at the selling price for an item of which we know the cost price, we use the following formula:

Selling price = Cost price divided by (100–Margin)/100

Thus, if cost price = £1000 and our desired margin = 35%, then Selling Price = £1000 divided by 0.65, or £1538. Our margin is Profit (£538) divided by Selling Price (£1538) and multiplied by 100 which comes to 35%.

A Gross Margin of 30% is towards the bottom of the acceptable range. If you cannot achieve better than, at the least, 29%, you really should be in another business. Lots of companies struggle through at rates lower than this, but it is no fun. Your Gross Margin is all you have to defray all the costs of running your business and to provide a proper return for your shareholders, which in this case means you.

There is, perhaps, one case where this may not be so, and that is where you have received so large a redundancy payment that part of it is taxable. In this case, you may feel that running a business that makes only a small profit, or even a loss, during the first three years may be worthwhile as you will be able to carry the losses or unused tax allowances back and claim a refund of tax already paid. If you are in this position, seek the advice of a good accountant, who will get you an advance ruling from the Inland Revenue in order to make sure that there are no unpleasant surprises. I will not advise you here. There are some points worth making, though, and they are these. Would you not rather make a profit than a loss? And what happens at the end of three years – do you wind up the business? Or do you then try to raise prices in order to turn a marginal business into a profitable one? And will your customers let you?

How much are your materials and goods for sale going to cost you?

How much will you need to pay your staff?

What prices are your competitors charging?

If you sold at precisely their price levels, what margins would that give you? Is that enough? If not, can you negotiate a better deal from your suppliers?

When you have answered all these questions, you have the basis of a Business Plan. Write it all down. If the Plan demonstrates that you cannot, in fact, carry out the business you had in mind with any real hope of success or profit, review the figures. If you still cannot make them work, drop the idea now. Look for something else. Otherwise, remember that you have not carried out this exercise for nothing; this Plan describes the way you are going to run your business. Do not deviate from it in the future without good reason, and without thinking through the effects. This will include updating the Cash Flow Forecast (see below) to assess the impact of the proposed change.

Here are two examples of the kind of change that new entrepreneurs believe to be forced upon them, but which they should really examine more closely before agreeing.

---

## Example 1

The owner of a new business has set list prices on the basis of a 40% gross margin for small transactions; a sliding scale of discounts for bulk business takes this margin down in stages to a low – for sales of more than £100,000 p.a. – of 30%. Careful examination of her costs has convinced the owner that a margin of 30% is the absolute minimum that will allow her to cover them and still retain any net profit from the transaction.

She is offered an order worth £12,000, but the customer demands a bigger discount than the largest she has contemplated – one which will take the gross margin down to 25%. The customer's justification for this demand is that such a discount will bring the price to a point sufficiently far below that charged by the existing supplier to make a change worthwhile.

Many new businesses will accept the order, on the basis that 25% is better than nothing, and that they need the turnover. Am I really saying that this order should be turned down? Yes, I am. If 25% is below the minimum margin needed to make a profit, it is *not* better than nothing – it is emphatically worse. Many deals like this one, and our new company will soon be among the bankruptcy statistics. One of the hardest lessons for new entrepreneurs to learn is that there really is business which should be turned away – even when it appears to be profitable. Your Business Plan, if you remind yourself of the reasons behind the various decisions it represents, will help you make these tough – but correct – decisions.

## Example 2

A new company is in business to sell computer equipment of a specialised type. Market Research shows that there is a market large enough to support the company, and that the market niche addressed is small enough not to attract the very large players who could swamp the new enterprise before it got going.

A very large company tells the owner of the new business that they have another supplier for the product he is selling, but that they might be interested in another device which is not on common sale. They hint that this would be a good place for the new company to start, and that success with the new device – which sells for about £1,200 and of which the company needs fewer than 10 – might be the way into the other, more lucrative business.

What typically happens is that the new entrepreneur invests a great deal of time and effort in sourcing the new device, in the hope that it will lead to bigger things. Our advice is that you do not do this, and the Business Plan is where you will find the strength to take this advice. You planned your business on a given product. You satisfied yourself that the market for that product was big enough. If you are right, then the 'numbers game' of selling will prove it. You must call on enough potential customers, essentially saying: 'This is what I've got. Are you interested?' If the information behind your Business Plan was correct, you will get enough takers. If you do not – then your market research was faulty. In any case, you are not going to survive by selling equipment worth £12,000; and my experience is that the other business which was hinted at does not arrive. Furthermore, you have wasted a great deal of time which would have been better spent on promoting your core business.

So re-read your Business Plan, and stick to it.

**Cash Flow Forecasts.** It is entirely possible to trade profitably, and yet to go bankrupt. This is often difficult for non-businesspeople to understand; but it is true. The reason is that profits are not necessarily translated into cash. Here is a simplified example of what happens.

ABC Engineering Ltd is set up by John Smith with working capital of £1,000 in cash. It obtains an order worth £600, which John Smith has priced as follows:

| | |
|---|---|
| Raw materials | £200 |
| Labour costs | £200 |
| Delivery costs | £20 |
| Profit | £180 |

This represents a gross margin of 30% (180 divided by 600 and multiplied by 100) and John Smith is very happy to take it on. That 30% is more than enough to cover his £80 in overheads and still leave him with a net profit (i.e., net after all expenses) of £100.

Immediately after he ships the finished goods, his Balance Sheet looks like this:

| LIABILITIES | | ASSETS | |
|---|---|---|---|
| Invoices payable | £300 | Cash | £800 |
| (£200 for materials, | | | |
| £80 for overheads, | | | |
| £20 for delivery costs) | | Receivables | £600 |
| Net Profit | £100 | | |
| Shareholders' Funds | £1000 | | |
| Total | £1400 | | £1400 |

NOTE: Cash stands at £800 (£1000 - £200) because John Smith paid his labour costs in cash. Also, an engineering company would, of course, require more capital and would have assets like machinery and tools, but this example is intended to be simple.

Now, he takes on a new contract. The figures on this are:

| | |
|---|---|
| Sale price | £1200 |
| Raw materials | £400 |
| Labour costs | £400 |
| Delivery costs | £50 |

Clearly, the gross margin on this deal is £350 (£1200-£850), or 29%, and John Smith is even more delighted. Because he is a new company with no credit record, his suppliers of raw materials and shipping demand payment of their existing invoices before extending new credit, but this amounts to only £300 including overheads – fuel, postage, rent and so on – and the company has £800 in the bank, so this is no problem.

After this second deal, the Balance Sheet looks like this:

| LIABILITIES | | ASSETS | |
|---|---|---|---|
| Invoices payable | £450 | Cash | £100 |
| (£400 for materials, | | | |
| £50 for delivery costs) | | Receivables | £1800 |
| Net Profit | £450 | | |
| Shareholders' Funds | £1000 | | |
| Total | £1900 | | £1900 |

Two contracts successfully completed, labour and overheads paid for, invoices payable kept current, and £450 already in the Profit and Loss Account! Wow! John Smith always knew that he was cut out for business, and his only regret is that he did not do it years ago.

And now he wins his third contract! A smaller one than before, but still business. The terms look like this:

| | |
|---|---|
| Sale Price | £500 |
| Raw Materials | £130 |
| Labour costs | £180 |
| Delivery costs | £15 |

The gross margin has shot up to 35%, for a number of reasons – he knows more about the manufacturing process now, and so is able to make more economic use of both labour and raw materials; as a bigger buyer he has negotiated a better raw materials contract, and the transport company has also improved his terms. ABC Engineering Ltd. is really going places.

The only drawback is that he still has to settle his existing accounts payable, amounting to £450, he has labour costs of £180 to meet, and new operating costs of £40 are due. A total of £670 – and he has only £100 in the bank.

He approaches the bank for assistance – and they turn him down because of his short trading record and lack of security. He asks his customers to settle their invoices – but they make it clear that they are accustomed to taking more than sixty days to pay, even though ABC's credit terms call for payment in thirty days. The company is in deep trouble. It cannot meet overheads, like rent, that need to be paid if it is to stay in business. It cannot pay its employees. And it cannot accept the new contract. And yet it has been trading profitably! What on earth can have happened?

The answer, in a nutshell, is that ABC Engineering Ltd has been overtrading. When it began, it needed working capital to enable it to buy raw materials, pay the labour and other costs to convert these into finished goods, cover shipping costs and overheads, and then to carry the level of Accounts Receivable that its sales generated until they were paid. It simply did not have enough of this working capital, and so it demonstrated the truth of one of business's paradoxes – that you can operate profitably and still go bankrupt; because bankruptcy is not about profit, but about the inability to pay bills as they fall due.

Cash Flow Forecasts show the planned inflows and outflows of cash each month, and avoiding the sort of situation we have just outlined is one reason for preparing them. Another is to show whether or not the Business Plan is realistic at all. A third, and possibly in practice the most frequent, is that we are going to need to raise some additional capital and the lender wants to see cash flow projections before committing himself.

Begin with a piece of paper arranged sideways on (i.e., long side horizontally). Leave a wide column to the left in which to write the nature of the inflows and outflows, and then to the right draw a series of columns to represent the months. It should look like this:

| Item | Month 1 | Month 2 | Month 3 | Month 4 | Month 5 | And so on |
| --- | --- | --- | --- | --- | --- | --- |

Now begin to enter the items you believe you will spend. Some of them may be definite – for example, if you have rented premises and leased a van, the costs will be known – but many will be based solely on your forecasts. One trap you must beware of is rigging the figures to give the result you are looking for. It you are not wholly honest with yourself at this point, you risk financial disaster in the future. *And do not be too optimistic.*

All of this is a whole lot easier, by the way, if you can use a personal computer. Microcomputer programmes like Lotus 1-2-3, Symphony and Excel are known as "electronic spreadsheets" and are simply computerised versions of the sheet of columns that we have been describing here, but they are much easier to change or update, and they do allow you to ask "What-if" questions – *What if sales are 50% lower than forecast? What if we have to cut the price by 20% to meet competition? What if our costs rise by 10% after four months?* – and so on.

This has been a very simple example, of course, but it has illustrated the important concept that you can trade profitably and still go bankrupt; if John Smith had prepared a cash flow in advance it would have demonstrated very clearly how disastrously underfunded ABC Engineering Ltd was, with the money supply running out after only three weeks, and no possibility of relief until the first invoice was settled in Week 8 – by which time the cash deficit would be enormous. A Profit and Loss Forecast prepared for this four-week period would have shown a healthy profit, but a Cash Flow Forecast would have shown that the business had insufficient cash reserves to complete the proposed transactions.

Even from such a simple example, then, the non-accountants among us can learn three things: that profit and cash flow are not the same thing; that it is cash, and not profit, that oils the wheels of business; and that you really can go bankrupt while making a profit.

## Figure 9.1: *British Coal Enterprise Cash Flow Forecast (Form PDC907)*

Cash Flow Forecast    for...........................................    For the period from......................to..........................

(name of company, firm etc)    Date when forecast prepared..................................

| | BUDGET | ACTUAL | BUDGET | ACTUAL | BUDGET | ACTUAL |
|---|---|---|---|---|---|---|
| ENTER PERIOD (monthly) | | | | | | |
| **RECEIPTS** | | | | | | |
| REVENUE ITEMS | | | | | | |
| Collections from debtors | | | | | | |
| Cash Sales | | | | | | |
| Other Income | | | | | | |
| Commissions | | | | | | |
| Rent | | | | | | |
| Investment Income | | | | | | |
| Repayment of VAT | | | | | | |
| Repayment of Corporation Tax | | | | | | |
| Other – Specify 1 | | | | | | |
| 2 | | | | | | |
| CAPITAL ITEMS | | | | | | |
| Net proceeds on disposal of assets | | | | | | |
| Loans Received | | | | | | |
| Capital Grants | | | | | | |
| Capital Introduced | | | | | | |
| **TOTAL RECEIPTS A** | | | | | | |
| **PAYMENTS** | | | | | | |
| REVENUE ITEMS | | | | | | |
| **Trading Expenses** | | | | | | |
| Payments to Trade Creditors | | | | | | |
| Cash Purchases | | | | | | |
| Gross Wages (including NHI) | | | | | | |
| **Administration Expenses** | | | | | | |
| Gross Salaries (including NHI) | | | | | | |
| Directors' Remuneration | | | | | | |
| Rent | | | | | | |
| Rates | | | | | | |
| Insurance | | | | | | |
| Repairs and Renewals | | | | | | |
| Heat, light & power | | | | | | |
| Hire & Leasing charges | | | | | | |
| Printing & stationery | | | | | | |
| Legal & Professional | | | | | | |
| Postage & telephone | | | | | | |
| Vehicle running costs | | | | | | |
| Entertaining & travelling | | | | | | |
| Selling & Distribution | | | | | | |
| Advertising | | | | | | |
| Carriage & packing | | | | | | |
| Finance costs | | | | | | |
| Loan interest | | | | | | |
| Bank charges | | | | | | |
| CAPITAL ITEMS | | | | | | |
| Capital Purchases | | | | | | |
| HP Instalments (including interest) | | | | | | |
| Loan repayments | | | | | | |
| OTHER PAYMENTS | | | | | | |
| VAT | | | | | | |
| Corporation Tax | | | | | | |
| Dividends | | | | | | |
| Sundry | | | | | | |
| **TOTAL PAYMENTS B** | | | | | | |
| Movement before overdraft interest [if B greater than A, show thus ( )] | | | | | | |
| Overdraft Interest | | | | | | |
| Net Movement | | | | | | |
| **OPENING BANK BALANCE C** | | | | | | |
| **CLOSING BANK BALANCE** | | | | | | |

# CASH FLOW WORKING PAPERS

| | P1 | P2 | P3 | P4 | P5 | P6 | P7 | P8 | P9 | P10 | P11 | P12 | TOTAL | Year 2 | Year 3 |
|---|----|----|----|----|----|----|----|----|----|-----|-----|-----|-------|--------|--------|
| | | | | | | | | | | | | | | Year 1 | £'000s |
| **Debtors** | | | | | | | | | | | | | | | |
| Opening Debtor Balances | | | | | | | | | | | | | | | |
| Sales Invoiced | | | | | | | | | | | | | | | |
| Cash Received | | | | | | | | | | | | | | | |
| Closing Debtor Balances | | | | | | | | | | | | | | | |
| **Creditors** | | | | | | | | | | | | | | | |
| Opening Creditor Balances | | | | | | | | | | | | | | | |
| Purchases | | | | | | | | | | | | | | | |
| Payments | | | | | | | | | | | | | | | |
| Closing Creditor Balances | | | | | | | | | | | | | | | |
| **Finished Goods Stock (Units)** | | | | | | | | | | | | | | | |
| Opening Balances | | | | | | | | | | | | | | | |
| Units Produced/Completed | | | | | | | | | | | | | | | |
| Units Sold/Despatched | | | | | | | | | | | | | | | |
| Closing Units of FGS | | | | | | | | | | | | | | | |
| Finished Goods Stock Value | | | | | | | | | | | | | | | |
| **Wages/Salary Costs** | | | | | | | | | | | | | | | |
| Direct Labour | | | | | | | | | | | | | | | |
| Indirect Labour | | | | | | | | | | | | | | | |
| Salaried Staff | | | | | | | | | | | | | | | |
| Directors | | | | | | | | | | | | | | | |
| **Cost of sales** | | | | | | | | | | | | | | | |
| Material of Sales Value | | | | | | | | | | | | | | | |
| Labour of Sales Value | | | | | | | | | | | | | | | |
| Total Cost of Sales | | | | | | | | | | | | | | | |

**Figure 9.2:** *British Coal Enterprise Cash Flow Working Papers*

## Profit and Loss Forecasts

| | Year 1 £'000 | Year 1 % | Year 2 £'000 | Year 2 % | Year 3 £'000 | Year 3 % |
|---|---|---|---|---|---|---|
| Sales Units | | | | | | |
| Value | | 100.00 | | 100.00 | | 100.00 |
| Direct Costs: | | | | | | |
| Materials | | | | | | |
| Labour | | | | | | |
| Total Direct Costs | | | | | | |
| Gross Profit | | | | | | |
| Overheads: | | | | | | |
| Direct Labour Variance | | | | | | |
| Indirect Labour | | | | | | |
| Salaried Staff | | | | | | |
| Directorate | | | | | | |
| General Overheads | | | | | | |
| Vehicle Leasing | | | | | | |
| Depreciation | | | | | | |
| Total Overheads | | | | | | |
| Operating Profit before interest | | | | | | |
| Bank Interest | | | | | | |
| Net Profit before Tax | | | | | | |
| Retained Earnings | | | | | | |

## Balance Sheet Projections

| | Year 1 £'000 | Year 1 % | Year 2 £'000 | Year 2 % | Year 3 £'000 | Year 3 % |
|---|---|---|---|---|---|---|
| **Fixed Assets** | | | | | | |
| Land & Buildings | | | | | | |
| Plant & Machinery | | | | | | |
| Less Depreciation | | | | | | |
| **Current Assets** | | | | | | |
| Stocks – WIP | | | | | | |
| - FG | | | | | | |
| Debtors | | | | | | |
| Bank | | | | | | |
| **Current Liabilities** | | | | | | |
| Creditors | | | | | | |
| Bank Overdraft | | | | | | |
| Net Current Assets | | | | | | |
| Capital Employed | | | | | | |
| **Represented by:** | | | | | | |
| Share Capital | | | | | | |
| Revenue Reserves | | | | | | |

**Figure 9.3:** *British Coal Enterprise Profit & Loss Forecast and Balance Sheet Projections*

If ABC Engineering Ltd. had prepared only a Profit and Loss Account, it would have been very optimistic about the future. If this had been supplemented by a Cash Flow Projection, the optimism – which is still justified because the company clearly can be profitable – would have been tempered by the realisation that a much greater cash investment would be required. To find out how much, it would be necessary to extend the Cash Flow Forecast a considerable way into the future, making the most cautious assumptions (for example, bringing forward the dates when cash must be paid out and pushing back the dates when receipts could be expected), until the point arrived at which the cash deficits began to shrink.

The maximum cash deficit revealed would show the scale of ABC Engineering Ltd.'s financing problem – because that is what it is. The company can be profitable – but it needs sufficient cash to enable it to operate.

Cash Flow Forecasts used in actual situations need to be rather more complex than the one we have just talked about, because real-life business is complex. To illustrate the depth to which planning must be taken, we are going to use the forms developed by British Coal Enterprise Ltd (BCE). BCE provides finance to new companies planning to create jobs in areas where redundant miners need them, and these projections are the ones they require before considering an application.

Figure 9.1 shows the Cash Flow Forecast that BCE loan applicants have to complete. It has been shortened horizontally, in that many more forecast periods are required, but all vertical headings are there, so, if it does nothing else, this form will draw your attention to the extent and variety of the kinds of payments that a business is likely to have to find. You will note that each month has two columns; one for budget, and one for actual. This enables you, at the end of each month, to enter against your forecast how the figures actually turned out, and thus to monitor your progress. You can then take steps to put right what is going wrong.

Figure 9.2 is the BCE Worksheet, designed to help you put the figures together for the Cash Flow Forecast, and Figure 9.3 provides projections of both your Profit and Loss Account and your Balance Sheet.

You will see that the planning involved in starting or running a business is considerable. For those not used to it, help is available.

The Training & Enterprise Councils (or Local Enterprise Companies in Scotland) provide a number of business support services. These include business planning kits, short part-time training programmes and seminars on topics including book-keeping, finance, marketing, together with business advice, counselling and information. Contact your local TEC for details.

As we have said, a Cash Flow Forecast allows you to establish how much money you are going to need to run the business. Where should this cash come from? We have included an Appendix on sources of funds for business.

**Business Plans revisited**. Let us now return to what is probably the single most important thing you have to do when planning to go into business for yourself – the Business Plan. Figure 9.4 lists the questions you must address when preparing a Business Plan. Reading these questions in order will make clear the position occupied by the Business Plan in the whole process of creating a business strategy; it comes after the Mission Statement – without which there is no clear base from which the Business Plan can be started – and before the Cash Flow and Profit and Loss Forecasts, which rely heavily on the Business Plan for input.

You may not be able to answer all of the questions in Figure 9.4 with authority, in which case you should consider using Market Research. There are three approaches to market research; they are, in order of increasing cost:

- Conversations with people already involved in the market but who are geographically sufficiently distant not to be your competitors;
- Published research from consultants specialising in your field;
- Market research carried out by a specialised agency and commissioned by you.

If you can find someone experienced *and successful* in the market who is prepared to give you free advice, fine. Take it. If not, you will need to consider the other options. Neither of these is cheap, but they cost less than ploughing everything you have and everything you can borrow into a business venture that fails for lack of information, leaving you penniless.

In many areas of business, there are specialist researchers and publishers who exist by selling the results of their researches. The Economist Intelligence Unit is a good place to start, not because they are likely to be able to provide you with exactly what you want, but because they can probably point you in the right direction for research on your chosen field. These research reports are not cheap – expect to pay anywhere from £250 or more for an annual newsletter subscription to several thousands of pounds for a specialist report. They may, though, cost less than the most expensive option, which is market research undertaken at your request and tailored to your specific needs.

Specialist market research firms, which are often allied to advertising agencies or management consultancies, have devised very effective ways of finding out what people want to buy, how much they would be prepared to pay for it, how it should be promoted, what features they require to see, and what features would be regarded as damaging to the prospects of sales. Their experience is such that they can help you to devise the best approach for information gathering in your selected market. An expenditure of a few thousand pounds here may save you losses of a great deal more. It will also help you provide your bankers with more credible information about your chances of success, and help to raise the capital you require.

If you do invest in market research, and the advice you receive is that your project is unlikely to succeed, do not ignore that advice. It has already cost you a lot of money; ignoring it could cost you a lot more. Find another field of endeavour, where your chances of success will be greater.

# BUSINESS PLAN QUESTIONNAIRE

*To fulfil your Mission Statement:*

What turnover must you achieve?
What existing competitors will you face?
What is their turnover?
How much can you charge for what you want to sell?
  How does that compare with:
       What it will cost you to make or to provide?
       What your competitors are charging?
What staff will you need when you are the size you aim to be?
  How much work can each staff member handle?
  How much unproductive travel will there be between contracts?
  How much will we have to pay them?
Where do you intend to get your business from?
  Will you win it from the existing number 1?
  Take it from smaller competitors?
  Find untapped markets?
How will you beat the competition?
  (a) By offering a better service?
    How good is their service?
    How will you better it?
    Where will you get your staff?
    How will you train them?
    How will you supervise them?
    What incentives can you offer them to do a better job?
  (b) On price?
    Can you afford to?
  What will you do if the competition responds with price cutting of its own?
How are you going to get your product to market?
Are you making something?
Growing something?
How are you actually going to make it?
  What machinery will you need?
  And what operators?
  Where can you find that machinery?
  And those operators?
  How much will they cost?

What about advertising and marketing?
   What do your competitors do?
   How effective is it?
   Can you think of good alternative methods?
   What will it cost?
How will you price your services?
How will you price your products?

**Figure 9.4:** *Questions to be answered when preparing Business Plan*

---

Make sure that you have discounted the "dream" elements of your desire for self-employment. Is your plan capable of achievement?

Examine carefully the list of qualities needed for success. Do you have them? *All* of them?

You *must* plan before you start. Planning means:

- Mission Statement
- Business Plan
- Cash Flow Forecasts

Calculate what your Gross Margin will be. If it is less than 30%, you probably do not have a workable plan.

You can trade profitably, and still go bankrupt. What matters is cash flow.

**Figure 9.5:** *Working for yourself – summary of major points*

---

# CHAPTER TEN

# Management Buyouts and Buyins

The management buyout was imported to this country from the USA, and has been a most successful transplant – judged only by the numbers of buyouts that have taken place. From a standing start in the late 1970s, more than a billion pounds bas been paid in buyouts during each of the three years 1986 to 1989.

If we examine the ultimate success or failure of the businesses involved, and the degree to which those involved have achieved the financial aims which, in many cases impelled them towards the buyout, we must conclude that the jury is still out. Rising interest rates have, inevitably, cast a pall over a means of buying companies using large amounts of borrowed money.

This is an introduction to Management Buyouts; it is a big subject and you should refer to a specialised book for a detailed treatment. One that deals very well with the complexities is: *Management Buyouts: Success and Failure away from the Corporate Apron Strings* by David Clutterbuck and Marion Devine, published by Hutchinson Business under ISBN 0-09-172270-5. Another is *The Management Buyout* by Spicer and Pegler.

If, after reading those books, you feel an interest in pursuing the idea of a buyout, ensure that you seek the soundest of financial and legal advice. Do not dream of entering into negotiations for a buyout purely on the basis of what is written here – you do need Clutterbuck and Devine's book, or Spicer and Pegler's, or both, and you do need specialist advice.

However, we will deal in this chapter with some of the more obvious features of the buyout.

A management buyout involves the purchase by the management team of a significant stake in their company which in almost all cases amounts to control of the company. The bought-out unit will very frequently be a subsidiary or a parent group, or a reasonably self-contained unit which is not part of the company's core business. The management's financial resources are usually very modest in relation to the sums involved, so that, unless the company is fairly small, most of the cash will come from outside investors.

In its extreme, but also probably its most common form, the buyout is a "leveraged buyout", where the bulk of the purchase price is financed through loans from banks, venture capital institutions, and other lenders. The ultimate objective will usually be to sell the company, either directly to a larger organisation or by floating it on the Unlisted Securities Market or on the Stock Exchange. Where this can be done successfully, the management team and the investors are likely to become very rich; but the debt load – particularly (as at the time of writing) in a time of high interest rates – can bring the company down.

The reason for taking part in a management buyout will probably be one of the following:

- The dream (which may be fulfilled) of making a lot of money;
- The desire to be in control;
- To resist a less attractive option, such as closure or sale of the business;
- Because your company, or your parent company, is in danger of passing into the hands of the receiver;
- Because your company, or your parent company, is government-owned and is to be privatised.

In Chapter 3, we discussed the qualities needed to succeed in business for yourself. Buying the company for which you work will mean that you are in business for yourself; and so the same qualities will be needed. You will, however, have some advantages, because you already know what business you are going to be in; you have experience of the market in which you will be operating; you know the strengths and weaknesses of your colleagues (and, if you are to succeed, some of them may well have to go) and also of your competitors; and, if your company has not been doing well, you may have some clear ideas on what to do about it.

Do you, though, know enough? Probably not. If you work for a publicly quoted company which regularly circulates high quality management accounting information, and if your position within the company is such that you are privy to the conversations, plans and concerns of managers in many different areas of the company, the information you have may be adequate.

What, though, if you do not have this depth of detailed knowledge? You must then make your first approach to your company's owners without sufficient knowledge on which to base proposals; and you would do well to remember what will at first seem surprising: that the initial buyout approach is often received extremely badly, may well be seen as disloyalty, and has on occasion been met with instant dismissal.

In any case, the road that leads to self-employment through management buyout must begin with an approach to find out whether the company is for sale. You would be wise at this point to appoint a professional adviser who specialises in buyouts; Clutterbuck and Devine's book will help you to find one.

Having overcome this first hurdle, you must now prepare your proposal. The first thing to do is to select a management team, and to distinguish between those who are to research and negotiate the buyout, and those who must keep the business working well while this is going on. Negotiations are likely to last for months, and it is only too easy for management eyes to be off the ball for this period. Competition will not be idle; and there is little point in establishing a first-class proposal for the financing of an entity which, because it has not been actively managed, is no longer in the same condition as when you started.

You are unlikely to be able to proceed directly to a set of financial proposals for presentation to bankers who may be interested in investing, but you should begin with a feasibility study, and you must be supported in this by your advisers. A great deal of what you are doing here is similar to the actions recommended in the previous chapter on Business Plans, with the proviso that you know a great deal about various areas of the questionnaire we asked you to consider there. The bulk of the cash flow projections will also be relatively easy, because you already know, or should know, what the relationship is between various items of expenditure, and what effect they have on income.

We referred earlier to the wide variations there may be in the amount of information you already possess. This is certain: that after your initial approach has established that the company, or your division, or whatever unit it is that you want to buy, is actually for sale, you are entitled to expect access to every detail that you require. Whether you will get this co-operation is questionable; but you must press hard for it.

This is particularly important because you will, of course, at some point have to agree the price you are going to pay. You would be unwise simply to accept the first figure named by the vendors, and you will only be able to form a view on the correct valuation of the company if you know all there is to be known about contracts, costs, income, asset values and encumbrances, redundancy costs, contingent liabilities and any other factors that your adviser will help you to establish.

While preparing your cash flow projections, you will need to examine the impact of borrowing, and to examine the effect of rises in interest rates. Because interest rates may already be high, do not assume that they can go no higher – they can.

It is entirely possible that you will find that a business that runs perfectly well when asset value is matched by equity does not work when it has to pay interest and capital on a large amount of debt. You may worry away at the figures, but still find that the numbers cannot be made to add up to a profit. This is not unusual. Despite the growing popularity – one might even say modishness – of buyouts, the great majority still never get beyond the feasibility study stage. Generating sufficient net profit to cover heavy interest payments is difficult, and many studies will show that, in this instance, it cannot be done. If yours is one of these, we recommend that you accept it. Management buyout teams are sometimes motivated by machismo, and ultimately came to grief. Neither machismo nor stubbornness is a good reason for proceeding with a bad idea.

It is at this, relatively early, stage that you should make your first contact with financial institutions, and Clutterbuck and Devine's book, together with your selected adviser, will help you to find them. You are not, at this stage, looking for a commitment of funds, but rather for confirmation that the potential investors like the early shape of your proposals and are likely to look kindly on an eventual approach for investment. They may also make suggestions about how you should frame those proposals, and about any changes they are likely to request in your approach.

If your investigations to this stage have not shown (and many – perhaps most – will) that your buyout cannot produce a business that will ultimately be successful enough to allow you to trade profitably, repay your indebtedness and realise your overall objectives, you are now ready to proceed to a detailed financial proposal. Once again, you will need the services of a skilled and experienced adviser who will help you to prepare a coherent and well-supported proposal and to negotiate with the banks on it.

If these negotiations are successful, you will not emerge with the money. What you *will* get is a verbal confirmation that the funds are likely to be available, if you can conclude a deal with the vendors along the lines indicated in your proposal. You are, therefore, now free to enter into firm negotiations for purchase of the business.

This may take a long time. As before, it is vital that the management team include people whose job is to negotiate, and others whose function is to keep the company running, as much as possible, as though nothing unusual were going on. You simply cannot afford not to pay full attention to the proper management of the enterprise.

We are not going to deal here with the mechanics of negotiation, any more than we have talked in detail about any of the other aspects of the buyout, because this is not that kind of book. You are entering a difficult and dangerous territory, and you need proper guidance. You will find it in the books of Clutterbuck and Devine, and Spicer and Pegler, and you should find it in your adviser. You must place yourself in their hands.

We will, though, say something about one more topic: the management buyin. While a buyout is the purchase of part or all of the business by those already working there, the buyin is a similar purchase by a management team currently employed elsewhere. Buyins are frequently hostile, in which case you will have to prepare your proposals without access to all the information you need.

The smaller company is often an excellent buyin target. It is well known that the management capable of building a business to a given size may not be the team that can take it successfully to bigger things. To take a specific example, a small team of engineers left their employer and started up a company making computer equipment in a fairly small way. The products were good and met a need, and the single factory was kept fully occupied with profitable orders.

Five years later, the company employed several thousand people. The products were still good, but:

- The plants were not run to full efficiency;
- New products were not developed as fast as market conditions demanded;
- Financial information systems were underdeveloped, so that incorrect management decisions were taken.

The problem was that the man who could run a single factory well was now Manufacturing Director responsible for five plants in three countries, and he did not have the skills to do that job. The good small company accountant was now Financial Director of a major undertaking, and he did not have the skills to do that job. The hands-on sales manager was now Sales and Marketing Director with a sales force in several countries, and his skills were at the same level as those of his colleagues.

Companies in this position have to bring in new, better-skilled management – or die. They should figure on the target list of any team of skilled managers looking for a company to buy.

A successful buyout is one that operates profitably, repays its debt and meets the personal objectives of the buyers. There have been many successful buyouts. And there have been many failures. Clutterbuck and Devine's book contains case studies of both. We recommend that you read it with close attention.

## CHAPTER 11

# *Voluntary work*

Early in this book, we identified voluntary work as something that would appeal to those readers who had neither the desire nor the financial need to go on working, but who were not ready to retreat to carpet slippers and warm fire. If you have no need to generate an income, but want to continue to experience the other satisfactions that people derive from work (self-esteem, peer group respect, a sense of belonging, friends, conversation), then working for the good of others may be just the thing for you. The Welfare State is not so all-encompassing that all of the needs of our society are, or even can be, met by full-time paid staff. There will always be a need for ordinary people to be involved on a voluntary basis.

The Appendices contain some addresses that will help you to find the agency that needs precisely what you have to offer. One of the things that make this such a rich field for the person in middle life who seeks new opportunities is that the range of needs is enormous – all the way from people able and willing to engage in hard physical labour to those who can be trained to provide loving support to the bereaved. Examine your own talents in the light of this chapter and decide what you could do.

And here is a warning: do not imagine that, because you are going to be unpaid, you should give the choice any less attention than if you were look-ing for paid employment, or expect to work any less hard while you are actually there.

The range of possibilities is huge. So huge, that it is difficult to know how one is to choose. So huge, on the other hand, that there is certain to be something that you can do, that you will want to do, and that fits in with your needs. You thought voluntary work was about helping to meet other people's needs? It is; but your needs are also important, and if you fail to take them into account, you will not end up with long-term satis-faction. Before you approach any organisation, work out answers to the following questions:

- How many hours a week do you want to work?
- When would you like those hours to be scheduled?
- During what hours do you really not want to be working?
- What skills do you have that a voluntary organisation might find a good use for?
- What satisfactions – meeting people, conversation, the chance to use a special skill – would you like to get from your voluntary work?

Only when you have the answer to these questions are you in a position to begin your search for suitable work. And, as we said, the possibilities are endless.

If you are a gardener, did you know about Horticultural Therapy? This charity, based at Goulds Ground, Vallis Way, Frome, Somerset, BA11 3DW, exists to promote gardening clubs for handicapped and disadvantaged people.

Or how about the Rambler's Association, whose paid officials are not numerous enough to walk along and check the condition of every recognised footpath? Then there is the Abbeyfield Society, which provides homes for elderly residents and is always in need of people to administer, shop, garden, drive or carry out the many other functions needed by such an organisation.

We have provided a list of addresses you may wish to contact in an Appendix to this book. The local library will have details of local voluntary groups. So will the local Citizen's Advice Bureau. So will the local Volunteer Bureau or Council of Voluntary Service (look under "V" for volunteer in your telephone directory).

Also at your local Reference Library, you will find an excellent book called *The Voluntary Agencies Directory*. This lists nearly 2,000 voluntary agencies, with details of what they do, where they are, what sort of people they require and how to contact them. The book is published by the National Council for Voluntary Organisations whose address and telephone number are in the Appendix, along with those for the Scottish Council for Voluntary Organisations and the Wales Council for Voluntary Action.

Additionally, there is a specialist recruitment agency called Charity Recruitment dealing with voluntary organisations. It is at The Garden Studios, 11-15 Betterton Street, London WC2H 9BP, telephone 071-379 0344.

# CHAPTER 12

# *Further Education*

Is there, somewhere in the back of your mind, a nagging feeling that your education in some areas has been neglected? People are curious by nature, and they strive for achievement, and the desire for education can grow stronger in the middle years. University is not only for the young; the number of mature students is growing. Nor need you feel restricted to the Open University – the particular pleasures that come from being part of a more conventional student body can still be enjoyed. Do not imagine that you will be the only mature student there – you won't.

You have no need to work full-time again. Perhaps some voluntary work, to help those less fortunate than you; perhaps some part-time work, for the interest and a little money. Your main objective, though, lies elsewhere.

Although you have been successful at work, you may still identify yourself as one of the millions whose potential has been at least partly wasted because you did not get the education that your intelligence deserved. Perhaps there are areas of interest that you have never been able to satisfy, because you were too busy. Perhaps you have an interest – in gardening, say, or reading – that you would now like to take further through a degree in Botany or English. Or perhaps a qualification will get you into a new line of work that you want to pursue.

The reason does not matter. The desire is enough.

So how do you go about it? It could not be easier. What do you want to do? A simple practical course, or a degree? There are courses in everything you can think of, at every level you can imagine – and if there is no suitable course locally, try 'distance learning' (the modern name for what we used to call correspondence courses).

Go to your local library. Ask for a list of local colleges, and contact them for prospectuses. And do not imagine that you are restricted to evening classes; there are plenty of mature students attending 'A' level courses in Sixth Form Colleges.

Also at the library are the prospectuses for the Universities, and here, once again, mature students are growing in numbers. If you have never taken a degree before, the Local Authority is obliged to pay your tuition costs – every person in this country, however aged, is entitled to take a degree. Whether they will also pay some of your living costs depends on your financial position, but fill in the form anyway; you may be surprised. And remember: you do not have to be studying something useful. It does not have to lead to a productive new job. Education need not be "for" anything, except the satisfaction you get from exercising your brain, and learning what you want to do.

---

# POSTSCRIPT

A well-known broadcaster finishes his talks with the words, 'If you have been, thank you for listening.' If you started at the beginning of this book and read through to the end – thank you. I hope you found it interesting.

If, on the other hand, you knew at page 1 what it was you wanted to do, and dipped only into those chapters that you thought would help you – I still hope you found it interesting.

One hundred years ago, when Britain was in the grip of the Industrial Revolution, life for most people was hard. The challenges they faced – poverty, hunger, precariousness of employment, the lack of the welfare safety net – have largely been tackled.

So is life easier for us in the last decade of the twentieth century? Clearly, it is – in the basic matters of staying alive and providing for our families. In other ways, though, the challenges, though different, are as great as ever they were. This book is intended to help you plot your way through those difficulties. We hope you will feel that it has succeeded.

# APPENDIX ONE

## SOURCES OF FUNDS FOR BUSINESS

There are many possible sources. Shareholders' own funds must always provide a great deal of the financing, and for a good reason. Banks and other lenders like to know that the person to whom they are lending is deeply committed to the success of the enterprise; and there is nothing like a strong monetary involvement to strengthen that commitment.

People with good ideas, or businessmen without adequate funding, often complain that lending institutions have let them down – that the Banks do not know a good idea when they see one, or cannot understand how easily a loan can turn disaster into triumph. This is to misunderstand the nature of banking – banks lend their depositors' money, not their own, and their first duty is to their depositors. They exist to provide the money that oils the wheels of well-run commerce – not to speculate. If this is sometimes interpreted as meaning that banks will lend only to those who do not need to borrow, so be it. The lesson for every would-be entrepreneur must remain this: that the money most at risk in your business will be your own.

The first step in arriving at a financing plan is to assess how much you are going to need. Do this as follows:

**Step 1.** Find out the cost of all the equipment you are going to need.

**Step 2.** Draw up a Cash Flow Forecast, as previously discussed. Make the most pessimistic assumptions about when cash will have to be paid out, and when it will be received. Do not bank on anything happening more favourably than it might – you may well be wise to allow an extra two months or so before the money starts coming in, to allow for over-optimistic sales forecasts and production problems, and you had better assume that suppliers are going to want your money in 30 days. Remember the difference we brought out between cash flows and profit. Your cash balance will fluctuate. What is the largest negative balance revealed by the forecast? Add 20% to this figure, as a provision against the setbacks you cannot foresee but which will happen.

**Step 3.** How much do you need to live on each month? Do not fudge. Multiply the sum by the number of months during which the Cash Flow Forecast shows that the company will not be able to cover its own costs. Add another 20%, for the reasons given in Step 2.

**Step 4.** Add together the sums obtained in Steps 1, 2 and 3. This is the amount of cash you need before you commit yourself to the world of the self-employed.

Now, you do not have to provide all of this money in cash yourself. Some you may be able to borrow, some you may raise by taking other investors into the company, and the balance is what you must find.

How much? You will need to have at least half of the total that you are going to need before you approach lenders or investors. Regard this half as a guideline and as a minimum; if you cannot provide fifty per cent of your requirements from your own resources, you are unlikely to be able to motivate others to put up the balance. As we have already said, it is not enough that you have a good idea; if things go wrong (and they will), lenders and investors want to know that they can count on your deep-seated sense of commitment to the business. Nothing – other, possibly, than threatening to shoot you – has yet been designed that gives a greater assurance of that commitment than the knowledge that your money is on the line with everyone else's. In fact, your money will be on the line *before* everyone else's, because the shareholders are the last people to be paid out when a business collapses.

Your share of the money will come from your savings, your redundancy pay, and the equity in your house. Do not forget, then, that you can lose everything you have built up. When banks take mortgages against houses to support business loans, they do not do it for fun. They will not let you off because you are a sporting fellow, or because you nearly succeeded, or because your MP makes a fuss. If they cannot recover their loans any other way, they will sell your house – and you will not be in it at the time.

There are two concepts – gearing, and interest cover – that we need to address now.

Gearing is the ratio of borrowed funds to equity, which is best regarded as share capital – the stake that the proprietors, or shareholders, have in the business and which is not available to be withdrawn easily. Thus, share capital is equity, and a temporary loan that the shareholders have put in to cover a specific short-term need is not. Retained earnings – profits that have been earned and kept in the business – may be regarded as equity, but it must be clear that they are not about to be paid out as dividends.

An ideal gearing for the new company would be 1:2; in other words, equity would be twice the amount of borrowed funds. The lowest to which you should allow gearing to fall would be 1:1 – shareholders funds exactly matching borrowings. Below this, lenders will simply not feel that you have enough invested in the business.

Why? Because of the reasons given above; and also because of our second concept, interest cover. When a business depends too heavily on borrowed money, the interest payments start to strangle it. Ideally, interest cover should be at least 2, which means that net trading profits, before interest and Corporation Tax, should be twice the total of interest payments.

Now for the third concept: Limited Liability. You will be familiar with companies that have the work 'Ltd' as part of their name. Only a company that has gone through the legal process known as "incorporation" – which means that the company has become a separate legal entity, or "person" – is allowed to use the word 'Ltd', and it is an offence for any such company not to use it.

Anyone setting up a business that has not been incorporated – whether a sole trader or a partnership – is personally liable for all debts of the business. Thus, if Joe Smith is a plumber and calls his business Acme Plumbers, without incorporating it, then if it fails owing a lot of money, he, Joe Smith, will himself have to repay every penny that is owed. This sort of risk would have made it very difficult for businesses to grow, because no one would have taken risks, and risk is the lifeblood of business. So, Limited Liability companies came into being.

A Limited Liability company is one that has become a separate legal entity from its founders, and their liability for its debts is limited to the amount (if any – and there usually is none) unpaid on the shares they own. So, if Joe Smith turned Acme Plumbers into Acme Plumbers Ltd, with a share capital of £1,000, and if, as is usual, he paid up the whole of the £1,000, then he would not be personally liable for any debts of the company. (To do this, he would need a lawyer, and so will you. Get one by asking your bank manager to recommend one.)

There is another type of limited company – the public limited company, or plc. This is simply a limited company whose shares are traded on a recognised stock exchange. Before obtaining this listing, you will need to satisfy the stock exchange authorities on a considerable number of points, and to publish detailed information in the required form. You will require the help of an experienced advisor.

**Sources of equity.** This will usually be primarily yourself. Do you, though, have any contacts – friends, relatives or otherwise – who would like to take a stake in your business? You will have to give them some shares, of course, and this may be a problem in the long run. How well do you know them? Will you be able to get along together? Do you see things the same way?

Also, do you know anyone with proven business skills who would like to become a director of your company, putting up both capital and expertise? Perhaps, for example, your business is going to be heavily dependent on marketing, and you know nothing about the subject. Now you are in the same position as a potential lender – you will feel happier about following advice from someone who has a financial interest in the company's survival.

If you do believe that you will be able to attract outside finance, the Government has introduced the Business Expansion Scheme (BES), which gives tax benefits to people investing in a British business. Details are available from your local Tax Office, although your accountant (yes, you are going to need one of those, too, and you should find him the same way as you did your lawyer) will be a better source of advice. Briefly, though, an individual who can show that he is not one of the proprietors can get tax relief at his highest rate on an investment of up to £40,000 provided that this money goes into new ordinary shares – newly issued, not new to him – of an unquoted company.

Many accountants are skilled at setting up BES plans to bring investors and businessmen together, and yours may be able to help here. Like Venture Capital companies (see below), such investors are likely to want eventually to realise a large capital gain by seeing the company sold or floated on the Stock Exchange or Unlisted Securities Market, but is this a problem? One of the few ways to make a lot of money legally is to build up a company and then sell it. Could their objective not also be yours?

Banks and other lending institutions invest in equity. Ask your bank manager whether his bank has a subsidiary interested in this kind of investment.

We have included in another Appendix a number of other institutions who are also interested in equity investments, but we should mention venture capital here. Venture capital organisations exist to invest in the equity of promising companies. Many of them have specific interests, such as investing only in high tech companies. They will take a shareholding, and will insist upon having their own representatives sitting as directors on your board. You will have to comply with some fairly strict requirements in the matter of monthly, quarterly and annual reports, and the agreement will contain provisions as to what happens if the business does badly – you may, in the last resort, find yourself pushed out of your own company if more capital is needed and you cannot provide your share. Venture capital companies are interested in the capital gain that comes when the company they have invested in is sold. You may find it a little dispiriting to know that experience has led venture capitalists to this rule of thumb: that only one investment in ten succeeds on a large enough scale to enable them to be floated.

**Expansion Capital.** Before we get on to the sources of the other funds you may need, a word about expansion. If the business does well, it will grow. Business is a very competitive arena. Growth may be forced upon you as a means of survival.

So, what of expansion? Growth requires money. You may need new equipment, you may need new premises, you may need new vehicles. If you prepare a new cash flow forecast, you will certainly find that you need more working capital – the amount you are owed will increase, stocks of work in progress and finished goods will grow, and the cost of materials will grow.

Where are these extra funds to come from? There are two sources – internal, and external.

Growth funded internally is especially satisfying. What this means is that

110

you are earning profits, you are retaining them in the business, and you are using these funds to expand. In practice, you are likely to need both internal and external funding. Unless the business is generating profits, it is unlikely that external funds will be available – partly because it would make your gearing unacceptable. External sources of funds will be as for the initial start-up; but you are likely to find that lenders who were reluctant to get involved with an untried new business are more receptive when they have profit and loss accounts for two or three years to look at.

**Sources of funds other than equity.** As well as equity financing, you are likely to need three other kinds: short-term, or working capital loans; medium term loans; and long-term loans. Let us look at all three separately.

Working capital is, briefly, the money you need to finance receivables and stocks. Here is a sample (and simple) Balance Sheet:

| LIABILITIES | | ASSETS | | |
|---|---|---|---|---|
| | | | £ | £ |
| Accounts payable | 12,000 | Cash | | 1,520 |
| | | Accounts receivable | | 22,000 |
| | | Stock | | |
| | | Raw materials | 2,000 | |
| | | Work in progress | 5,000 | |
| | | Finished goods | 4,000 | 11,000 |
| Medium Term Loan | 4,000 | Fixed Assets | | 12,000 |
| Retained earnings | 13,520 | | | |
| Paid up capital | 17,000 | | | |
| TOTAL | 46,520 | | | 46,520 |

This is, as we said, a simple Balance Sheet, but it will illustrate what we want to say.

First, an observation about the nature of Balance Sheets: they show what the company owns, and how it is financed. In this case, the total assets (things owned) of the company amount to £46,520; the total liabilities (amounts owed) of the company must also be £46,520, because this is a Balance Sheet, and the two sides balance (are equal).

Of the total assets of £46,520, £34,520 are current assets – that is, they are assets that are regularly turning over in the course of business. Raw materials become work in progress and then finished goods, after which they are shipped to customers and transformed into accounts receivable which, when paid, become cash ready to be invested again into raw materials. A never-ending (we hope) cycle.

The remaining assets are fixed assets – plant, machinery, vehicles, premises; anything of a permanent nature needed so that the cycle of current assets can continue to operate.

On the liabilities side, current liabilities are those that need to be repaid in the short term. A bank overdraft would appear here, but the medium-term loan does not, so that the total of current liabilities amounts to £12,000. Medium-term liabilities are £4,000 and the remainder – share capital plus retained earnings (the profit that has been kept in the business, rather than paid away as dividends) represents the total of shareholders' funds.

Net current assets is the figure arrived at by deducting current liabilities from current assets, and in this case amounts to (£34,520-£12,000) or £22,520. This is a very healthy situation, because cash and accounts receivable together are equal to twice the total of accounts payable. Assuming that the company's debtors pay up on time, and that all of these receivables are good – that is, that they do not include significant sums due from people or companies who will not or cannot pay – there will be no problem in meeting payables from cash coming in.

This Net current asset figure is the company's working capital. If the company were not as liquid as it is (liquid means having sufficient cash or near cash [such as good receivables] assets), then it might need to look to outside lenders to provide working capital financing.

Suppose, for example, that we change the Balance Sheet a little, as follows:

| LIABILITIES | | ASSETS | | |
|---|---|---|---|---|
| | | | £ | £ |
| Accounts payable | 12,000 | Cash | | 1,520 |
| | | Accounts receivable | | 6,000 |
| | | Stock | | |
| | | Raw materials | 8,000 | |
| | | Work in progress | 9,000 | |
| | | Finished goods | 10,000 | 27,000 |
| Medium Term Loan | 4,000 | Fixed Assets | | 12,000 |
| Retained earnings | 13,520 | | | |
| Paid up capital | 17,000 | | | |
| TOTAL | 46,520 | | | 46,520 |

All that we have done is to move some of the company's assets from Accounts receivable to Stock. The working capital position remains the same, but the company is less liquid; it has only £7,520 in cash and accounts receivable to deal with accounts payable of £12,000. Although stock is a current asset, it is a good deal less "current" – less easily turned into cash – than accounts receivable. Finished goods have to find a buyer, be shipped and be invoiced, after which it will be at least 30 days – the average is more than 45 days – before we see the money. Work in progress has further to go, and raw materials are at the very beginning of the process.

So, the company now has to choose between two ways of dealing with its accounts payable; it can put off paying them until it has the cash, or it can borrow the money to pay for them.

Let us assume that putting off payment is not a practical option. Perhaps the raw materials supplier will not send more until he has been paid; perhaps those to whom we owe money are threatening legal action; whatever the reason, the bills must be paid. The company most borrow.

This loan will be a working capital loan, and there are various options. The first is to approach the bank, present our Balance Sheet, Profit and Loss Accounts and Cash Flow forecast, and ask for an overdraft facility. Provided that we can demonstrate that the current assets are good – that the stocks are fairly valued, do not contain any old, obsolete or unsaleable items, and that buyers at the right price are likely to be found, and that the accounts receivable do not include large amounts that are uncollectable, the bank will probably want to lend against this Balance Sheet. It will be a short-term loan, but is likely to be set up as a revolving facility. In other words, provided that the bank can see that the account is turning over regularly, as current assets are turned into cash and current liabilities met, the overdraft will not be withdrawn.

Interest rates on overdrafts may be quite high – you may well find yourself paying 5% or more over Base Rate – and security will be taken. This is likely to include both a floating charge over all of the assets of the business, and your personal guarantee, which may or may not be supported by a charge over your home. Other countries manage these things a little better – in Canada, for instance, banks can make what are called 'Section 88 loans' which, under Section 88 of the Bank Act, are protected with a first charge over the stock that the money was lent to finance, and after that by the receivables into which the stock is converted when sold, but, even in Canada, supporting personal guarantees are usually taken. Banks exist to finance good business, not to gamble with their depositors' money.

Factoring is another source of working capital finance. It involves, in effect, the transfer of your invoices to a specialist factoring company, which charges you interest on the money. This interest is described as 'discount', and factoring money will be at least as expensive as a bank overdraft. Factoring may be with or without, but in practice is most likely to be with, recourse. This means that you have not sold your invoices outright; if the factoring company does not obtain the money from your customer, it will ask you for it.

There is a list of factoring companies in another Appendix, but ask your bank manager if his bank has a subsidiary in the business.

**Medium and long-term loans.** Longer term assets require longer-term financing, if only on the basis that you should pay for an asset out of the money that it makes for you. So, for trucks, vans and other vehicles a financing period of one to three years is probably acceptable, while for expensive machine tools with a long life the figure may be five, seven or even more years, and for property, twenty years would not be unreasonable. We think nothing of buying a house on a twenty-five year mortgage, do we?

All of the major banks now offer medium-term financing, some also offer long-term money, and they all have subsidiaries that specialise in this sort of loan. They also have subsidiaries providing lease finance and hire purchase. Leasing may be a good way to obtain some of your fixed assets, but remember that you will never own the equipment. The Finance Houses are also very active in both the leasing and the hire purchase fields.

Other sources of term financing are mentioned in another Appendix.

**Regional (and other) grants.** Where are you? There are many different schemes to encourage the growth of industry in the less well-off areas. Ask your bank manager which you might qualify for and, if you are just outside a qualifying area – move!

In country areas, the Rural Development Commission provides loans of up to £75,000 for the purchase of property and equipment. In Scotland and Wales, the Scottish Development Agency (SDA) and Welsh Development Agency (WDA) do the same. The Department of Trade and Industry (DTI) provides grants, and will also put up money for such things as training, high tech feasibility studies, and consultancy to improve product quality, design and production techniques, and organisation. They are unlikely to find their way to your door; you have to go and ask them.

And don't forget that British Coal Enterprise is deep into the business of helping companies create employment in coal mining areas.

Export finance is a field of its own, and, if you intend to export, you should talk to your bank manager, as well as consulting the Appendix for firms specialising in financing the export trade. One name you must remember, though, is the Export Credit Guarantee Department (ECGD). The ECGD is not a financing organisation, in that it does not lend you the money to support export business. What it does is to insure your export invoices against non-payment, thus removing one of the greatest obstacles in the way of successful exporting. Talk to them before you ship the goods, not after.

# APPENDIX TWO

## USEFUL ADDRESSES

This appendix contains addresses that we hope will help you to find what you are looking for, and to locate help when you need it. It would have been easy to fill forty pages with such addresses, and we have resisted the temptation to do so. What you should find here are pointers to the source books and the organisations that will enable you to find what you want. We wish you good hunting, and a happy, satisfying, fulfilling future.

### Recruitment Consultants
(1) Check your local Yellow Pages.
(2) CEPEC, a commercial organisation, publishes CEPEC Recruitment Guide, obtainable from CEPEC Publications, Kent House, 41 East Street, Bromley, Kent BR1 1QC. This lists some 700 recruitment agencies in the UK.
(3) The Executive Grapevine; is a similar guide and is available from Executive Grapevine Ltd., 79 Manor Way, Blackheath, London SE3 9XG.

### Voluntary Work
The Voluntary Agencies Directory; is a book containing a comprehensive listing of nearly 2,000 Voluntary Organisations. It should be available at your local reference library, or can be obtained from Bedford Square Press, address as for the National Council for Voluntary Organisations.
National Council for Voluntary Organisations, 26 Bedford Square, London WClB 3HV. Tel: 071-636 4066.
Scottish Council for Voluntary Organisations, 18-19 Claremont Crescent, Edinburgh, EH7 4HX. Tel: 031-556 3882
Wales Council for Voluntary Action, Llys Ifor, Heol Crescent Caerfilli, Canol Morgannwg, CF8 1XL. Tel: 0222-869224.
Charity Recruitment is a recruitment agency for voluntary organisations. Address: The Garden Studios, 11-15 Betterton St, London WC2H 9BP.

### Your own business advice
(1) Ask your own bank whether it has a Small Business Advisory Service – most do.
(2) The Employment Department, Moorfoot, Sheffield, S1 4PQ. Also local branches.
(3) DTI Small Firms Centre. Centres are located in various cities around the country; to contact your local office, dial 100 and ask for FREEFONE Enterprise.
(4) Business in the Community, 227a City Road, London EC1V 1LX maintains a directory of Enterprise Agencies around the country.

## Financing

All High Street Banks provide overdraft and term loan facilities.

The Finance Houses Association, 14 Queen Anne's Gate, London SW1H 9AG, can supply details of their member companies who provide a wide range of industrial and business financing schemes.

Rural Development Commission, 35 Camp Road, Wimbledon Common, London SW19 4UP.

## Venture Capital

(1) British Coal Enterprise Ltd, Edwinstowe House, Edwinstowe, Notts NG21 9PR (tel: 0623 826804) provides venture capital and term loans to approved projects in coal mining areas.

(2) In addition to BCE and the major banks, there is a large number of venture capital providers in the UK. The following is a short selection. Business people looking for investment from those listed below are advised to retain specialist advisers first.

Abingworth plc
26 St. James's Street
London
SW1A 1HA

British Railways Pension Funds
50 Liverpool Street
London
EC2P 2BQ

Brown Shipley Developments Ltd,
Founders Court
Lothbury
London
W1M 0AL

CIN Industrial Investments Ltd
PO Box 10
London
SW1X 7AD

Scottish Development Agency
120 Bothwell Street
Glasgow
G2 7JP

Welsh Development Agency
Pearl House
Greyfriars Road
Cardiff
CF1 3XX

Investors in Industry Group plc (generally known as 3i)
91 Waterloo Road,
London
SE1 8XP

(3i is a large company owned jointly by the Bank of England and the clearing banks. It has a number of regional offices, and you can get the address of the one nearest to you by telephoning 071-928-7822.)

## Factoring

Lloyds, Midland and National Westminster Banks all have their own factoring companies, in addition to which there are a number of independent companies which can be found through the Yellow Pages.

## Leasing

All of the clearing banks have subsidiaries that provide lease finance. There is, in addition, a large number of other leasing companies which can be found through the Yellow Pages.

## Education

(1) Prospectuses from all British universities are available at your local reference library, who can also tell you where the local colleges of further education are. Your local Adult Education Institute will be in the Yellow Pages. For a list of Distance Learning, or Correspondence, Colleges contact the Council for the Accreditation of Correspondence Courses, 27 Marylebone Road, London NW1 5JS.

(2) Open University, Student Enquiries Office, PO Box 71 Milton Keynes, MK7 6AG.

## Investment

(1) Association of Unit Trusts, Park House, 16 Finsbury Circus, London EC2M 7JP.

(2) Association of Investment Trusts, Park House, 16 Finsbury Circus, London EC2M 7JP.

(3) British Insurance Brokers' Association, BIBA House, 14 Bevis Marks, London EC3A 7NT.

(4) Society of Pension Consultants, Ludgate House, Ludgate Circus, London EC4A 2AB.

(5) Financial Intermediaries, Managers and Brokers Regulatory Association (FIMBRA), 22 Great Tower Street, London EC3R 5AQ.

**Management Buyouts**

The following recommended books should be read before making any attempt to put together a management buyout. They include lists of advisers and investors.

> *Management Buyouts: Success and Failure away from the Corporate Apron Strings* by David Clutterbuck and Marion Devine, Hutchinson.
>
> *The Management Buyout* by Spicer and Pegler.

# INDEX

3i 117
Abingworth plc 116
Achievements 56, 62
Advertisements 39-46
Anger 9
Balance Sheet, Personal 31
Bereavement, similarity to redund-
    ancy 8
British Coal Enterprise Ltd. 1, 114,
    116
British Railways Pension Funds 116
Brown Shipley Developments Ltd 116
Business Expansion Scheme 110
Business in the Community 115
Business Plan 19, 84, 95
Cash Flow Forecast 19, 34, 88, 91, 113
CEPEC Recruitment Guide 53, 115
Change, reasons for 7
Change, through boredom 7
Change, through redundancy 7
Charity Recruitment 115
CIN Industrial Investments Ltd. 116
Computer printers 56
Curriculum Vitae 55
CVs 55
    CV as a selling document 55
    CV, mentioning age in 58
    CVs, achievements in 56
    CVs, binding 56
    CVs, content 58
    CVs, courses in 59
    CVs, educational qualifications in
        59
    CVs, format 55
    CVs, leisure interests in 59
    CVs, mentioning salary in 60
    CVs, profiles in 58
Depression 9
DTI Small Firms Centre 115
Employment Agencies 40
Factoring 117
Features, not benefits 57
Financial decisions 31, 36
Financial stresses 36

Further education 21, 105, 117
Further education, mature students 105
Gearing 108
Good boy file 75
Graphology 45
Grieving process 9
Handwriting 45
Headhunters, speculative letter to 53
Health 37
Hobby as full-time job 7, 18
Interviews as sales calls 55
Interviews, conduct in 76
Interviews, dress 75
Interviews, good boy file 75
Interviews, interviewer's objectives in
    76
Interviews, lines of questioning 76
Interviews, objection handling in 82
Interviews, preparation 72, 74
Interviews, punctuality 74
Interviews, questions about salary 79
Interviews, questions to ask 81
Interviews, research for 72
Investors in Industry Group plc 117
Job advertisements 39-46
Job applications, poor response to 55
Job Centre 38
Job Clubs 12
Job-seeker as salesperson 9
Kelly's Directory 46, 73
Kompass 46, 73
Lateral thinking 18
Leasing 117
Life, stages of 15
Local Education Authorities 18
Management Buyins 101
Management Buyouts 98, 118
Management Buyouts, leveraged 99
Margin 85
Market Research 95
Marketing Plan 19
Mature Students 105
Middle-age 15
Mission Statement 84

Mourning process 9
Moving house on retirement 17
National Council for Voluntary
  Organisations 115
Networking 38
Open University 105, 117
Overtrading 89
Paper quality 45, 55
Peer group respect 16, 28
People do not buy on rational grounds
  11
Personnel department 47
PLC, Annual Report 73
Positive Mental Attitude 12
Printers, computer 56
Psychological impact of redundancy 8
Psychometric tests 23
Reasons for change 14
Recruitment Consultants 38, 51, 115
Recruitment consultants, speculative
  letter to 53
Redundancy as bereavement 8
Redundancy as rejection 8
Redundancy, psychological impact of 7
Rural Development Commission 115
Salesperson, job-seeker as 9
Satisfactions from work 16, 26
Scottish Council for Voluntary
  Organisations 115
Scottish Development Agency 116

Second Chances for Adults 18, 30
Self-employment 7, 18
Shame at unemployment 12
Speculative approach 38, 46
Speculative approach, how not to
  write 51
Tests, psychometric 23
The CEPEC Recruitment Guide 53,
  115
The Executive Grapevine 53, 115
The Finance Houses Association 116
The Voluntary Agencies Directory
  104, 115
Time is not on your side 10
Typing 45, 56
Universities 117
Vocational Guidance 22
Voluntary Work 20, 104
Von Ludendorff 19
Wales Council for Voluntary Action
  115
Welsh Development Agency 116
Work, satisfactions of 16, 28
Working for yourself 84
Working for yourself, Limited Liability
  108
Working for yourself, sources of
  funds 107
Yellow Pages 47